THE STORY OF
JAPAN'S
OHMI
MERCHANTS

THE STORY OF JAPAN'S OHMI MERCHANTS

The Precept of *Sanpo-yoshi*

Kunitoshi Suenaga

Translated by Larry Greenberg

Japan Publishing Industry Foundation for Culture

Note to the reader:
All Japanese names appearing in this book are given in Japanese order, with family name first, with the exception of the jacket, case, title page, and photo credits. All dates have been changed to that of the Western calendar.

The Story of Japan's Ohmi Merchants: The Precept of Sanpo-yoshi
Suenaga Kunitoshi. Translated by Larry Greenberg.

Published by
Japan Publishing Industry Foundation for Culture (JPIC)
3-12-3 Kanda-Jinbocho, Chiyoda-ku, Tokyo 101-0051, Japan

First English edition: May 2019

This book is based on the book published in Japanese as *Ohmi shoningaku nyumon:CSR no genryu "sanpo-yoshi" kaiteiban* (Sunrise Publishing, 2017), which is a revised edition, first published in 2004 by the same publisher. The original text from the 2017 edition has been revised and edited by the author for the English version.

English publishing rights arranged with Sunrise Publishing.

Book design: Miki Kazuhiko, Ampersand Works

Printed in Japan
ISBN 978-4-86658-057-9
https://japanlibrary.jpic.or.jp/

CONTENTS

Preface to the English Edition

My research into the Ohmi merchants, who can be called the originators of Japanese-style management, seeks to better understand the unique aspects and universality of Japanese-style management by discovering, analyzing and compiling papers on the historical documents found in the former homes and warehouses of merchants.

The Ohmi merchants have a long history. In Japan, the mercantile industry made its first appearance around the twelfth century. From the very beginning, the farmers of the Ohmi region served as *zashonin* (Guild merchants) merchants who held special rights, and traded with the regions neighboring the Ohmi province during the agricultural off-season. The dedicated Ohmi merchants we know today appeared at the end of the sixteenth century. From that point onward, the Ohmi merchants expanded their trading territory throughout all of Japan, and even developed markets on the Asian continent and North and South America after the conclusion of trade treaties with the western powers in 1859. Today, many of the oldest companies in Japan can trace their roots to the Ohmi merchants.

In being chosen to become part of the "JAPAN LIBRARY" published by JPIC, *The Story of Japan's Ohmi Merchants: The Precept of Sanpo-yoshi* will be the first English-language publication in the long history of research into the Ohmi merchants. I am thrilled the achievements of the Ohmi merchants, which covered a vast geographical area and are still felt today, will now have a chance to be known throughout the world.

The original Japanese-language edition of *The Story of Japan's Ohmi Merchants: The Precept of Sanpo-yoshi* was written with the general public of Japan in mind, which meant many aspects of common knowledge in

Japan required no explanation. That knowledge is not common outside Japan, however, and I therefore thoroughly reviewed the text of the book for the English-language edition, revising difficult-to-understand passages, adding new passages to provide additional background not found in the original version, and giving annotations to aid greater understanding.

Long-term sustainability, rather than the pursuit of profit, forms the very essence of Japanese business. This point is starkly different from what is taught in U.S. university and graduate school business management courses, and may accordingly cause some initial bewilderment. That being said, while the principle of corporate social responsibility, CSR, is seeing increased adoption in businesses globally today, there is no doubt that some corporations outside Japan have also long adhered to principles similar to the *sanpo-yoshi* "three-way satisfaction" philosophy of the Ohmi merchants, who founded their practices on the tenets of Buddhism.

In presenting the achievements of the Ohmi merchants, who devoted themselves to organizational sustainability, refrained from charging high interest rates and placed the common good ahead of profit, it is my wish that this book will spark new interest in Japanese-style management and provide hints for the direction of business activities going forward.

Suenaga Kunitoshi

March 2019

Seiran-tei, Kyoto

The History of the Ohmi Region and the Rise of the Ohmi Merchants

Geography: Region Symbolized by Lake Biwa

Today, Tokyo is the capital of Japan, but until 1867, the capital was located in the city of Kyoto, where the emperor maintained his residence. Kyoto, then known as Heiankyo, became the capital of Japan in 794 and it remained the center of power for over one thousand years. Located to the east of ancient Kyoto is Shiga Prefecture, site of Lake Biwa, the largest lake in Japan. In the past, Japan was divided into sixty-six provinces, and what is now Shiga Prefecture was once known as Ohmi Province. The name "Ohmi" means the lake "closest to Kyoto." The lake is said to have gained its name from the similarity of its shape to the Chinese *pipa* lute, known as a *biwa* in Japan.

With a surface area of 693 square kilometers Lake Biwa makes up one sixth of the total area of Shiga Prefecture, whose total land surface area is 4,016 square kilometers. The lake, with a maximum depth of 103 meters, has two primary characteristics. First, while many lakes in Japan are caldera lakes formed in the mouths of collapsed volcanoes, Lake Biwa was formed by the shifting of

tectonic plates. It is also unique in that it is one of the few extremely ancient lakes in the world, having been formed five million years ago, shifting to its present location 1.2 million years ago. This makes the lake bottom a treasure trove of sediments and historical artefacts.

The Ohmi basin, centered on Lake Biwa, is surrounded by ranges of mountain over one thousand meters in height to the east, west

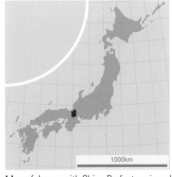

Map of Japan with Shiga Prefecture in red

and north and by relatively low mountains to the south. Approximately two hundred rivers and streams feed into the lake from these mountains, providing the local people with abundant water supplies for drinking, agriculture and industry. Lake Biwa can truly be considered the symbol of both the former Ohmi Province and modern-day Shiga Prefecture.

Only two rivers flow out from Lake Biwa, the Seta River, which originates at the Nango Weir on the southern side of the lake, and the Lake Biwa Canal, which flows towards Kyoto. Today, with a flood gate installed to control the flow of water to both the weir and canal, Lake Biwa serves as a reservoir of life to the fourteen million people living in the Kansai region.

History: A Tradition of Trade

Streams and rivers flow into Lake Biwa like a system of capillaries and arteries, starting from the mountainous regions and gradually joining together on the plains until they reach the lake. From ancient times, they have served as the source of life for all the people in the river basin. The inseparable relationship the people of the region had with Lake Biwa simultaneously created a distinct lifestyle and cultural sphere, giving rise to Ohmi's unique history.

From its very origins, Ohmi was a highly developed region bordering Kyoto, the center of political power. For that reason, the history of Ohmi is closely tied to the history of political, cultural, social and economic development in Kyoto.

Many of Japan's most historically important political events took place in Ohmi. In 667, the capital was transferred, though briefly, to Otsu in ancient Ohmi, and Otsukyo served as the stage for the greatest of ancient Japan's many wars of imperial succession, the Jinshin War, which broke out in 672. In 1221, the climactic battle of the Jokyu War, a massive clash between imperial courtiers and the warrior elite, ended in a decisive victory for the latter. The decisive battle of the war, which serves as the division between ancient and medieval Japan, was fought in the area of Setanokarahashi, the bridge crossing the Seta River flowing from Lake Biwa. During Japan's Warring States period (1467–1573), when powerful warlords (daimyo) clashed for suprem-

Lake Biwa

acy throughout the country, a free market edict (*rakuichi-rei*) was enacted in 1549 by Ohmi's daimyo Rokkaku Sadayori. The first of its kind, it was a pioneering piece of commercial policy, abolishing the special privileges held by powerful trade guilds and establishing the principle of free trade.

It was in Azuchi, in the central part of Ohmi, that Oda Nobunaga (1534–1582), the first of Japan's re-unifiers at the end of the Warring States period, built Azuchi Castle in 1576. And Sekigahara, a plain bordering the eastern edge of Ohmi, was where Tokugawa Ieyasu (1542–1616), the final victor of the wars of the period, fought his greatest battle in 1600. His victory enabled him to become shogun and establish his *bakufu* in Edo (present-day Tokyo) and ushered in the Edo period (1603–1867), an era of peace lasting for over 250 years.

Ancient Ohmi was first developed by immigrants from the Korean Peninsula and China, known as Toraijin (literally, people who have crossed over), who migrated in groups as a result of dynastic turmoil in their homelands. The Yamato court, Japan's ancient governing authority, had the Toraijin, who brought with them advanced technologies and culture, live in the area surrounding Lake Biwa and thus contribute to the development of the region.

Proof of their activities can be seen in the many place names in Ohmi that trace their origins to China and the Korean Peninsula, in the *kofun* burial mounds, and in the remains of temples and ironworks built by these first immigrants that can still be found throughout Ohmi.

Ohmi is the location of Enryakuji, the largest temple in Japan, of which

Oda Nobunaga

Reproduction of Azuchi Castle

Tokugawa Ieyasu

Konponchudo Hall, Enryakuji Temple

Hiyoshi Taisha Shrine

the emperor was a devout patron, built on the slopes of Mt. Hiei in 788 by the priest Saicho to provide spiritual protection for the capital from the potentially malevolent northeastern direction. Also located in Ohmi is Hiyoshi Taisha, the headquarters of the many Hiyoshi Shrines scattered throughout Japan. Many more temples and shrines of great history and pedigree can be found throughout Ohmi, and it is home to the third greatest number of old Important Cultural Properties in Japan, after the former capitals of Kyoto and Nara.

From a social and economic perspective, Ohmi, with the Ohmi basin and Lake Biwa serving as sources of abundant agricultural and aquatic resources, can be seen as a supply region of daily necessities for the many consumers in Kyoto, the center of political power at the time.

Ohmi was also a vital crossing point that connected Kyoto with eastern Japan. The intersection of the Nakasendo Road and the Tokaido Road, the most important routes connecting Heiankyo with eastern Japan, was located within its borders. Lake Biwa also served as a trade waterway to reach the Sea of Japan to the north. This vital traffic of people and goods led to the early development of organizations and individuals engaged in the concentrated delivery of vast quantities of products.

During the medieval period, local self-governing cooperatives, in which local farmers banded together to trade as a single unit, and trade guilds, which derived their exclusive rights to the sale and trading of specialized goods from the protective authority of Enryakuji and Hiyoshi Taisha, also thrived in the rural villages of Ohmi. Those rural people can be considered the first Ohmi merchants, setting out to engage in domestic trade with the neighboring provinces beyond the mountains surrounding the borders of Ohmi.

Japan's cities and commerce flourished during the country's isolation during the Edo period, founded on the peace which lasted from 1603 until the opening of trade with the West in 1859. The people of Ohmi expanded their trade beyond just the neighboring provinces to include all of Japan, travelling to Hokkaido in the north and to Kyushu in the south. These well-travelled merchants came to be known as "Ohmi merchants" in the lands they visited.

The prosperous cross-border trading that typified the business of Ohmi merchants continued after the Meiji Revolution in 1868, down to the outbreak of World War II, expanding to China and North and South America. Today, Japan boasts the largest number of companies with centuries-long histories in the world. Many of them, including general and textile trading companies in the trade industry, banking and insurance companies in the finance industry, and sake and soy sauce companies in the brewing industry, can trace their roots to Ohmi merchants.

The Rise of the Ohmi Merchants: The Three Elements of Heaven, Earth and People

Ohmi merchants, with their long eight-hundred-year history starting from the medieval period, can be considered the very source of Japanese-style management. Three key elements served as catalysts for their emergence. The first is the strong historical foundation that supported the growth of commerce in Ohmi, beginning with developments brought about by the Toraijin, with their advanced numeracy skills and technology, and further supported by the region's location next to the emperor's residence in Kyoto, bestowing the area with the social and economic role of supplier to the ancient capital.

The second factor is Ohmi's superb geographic location, being situated at nearly the very center of the Japan archipelago, and at the intersection of two of the most important roads in the country, the Tokaido and Nakasendo Roads that connected Kyoto with Edo. In addition to land transport, Lake Biwa provided ample water transport. Ohmi was thus an easy place to seize commercial opportunity, as key people, commodities and information were all sure to pass through its borders.

The third factor contributing to the ongoing emergence of prosperous Ohmi merchants is the strong social foundation formed over many generations by merchants who had attained success. These merchants did not relocate to major cities like Kyoto, Osaka or Edo after achieving wealth, but rather maintained their primary residences in Ohmi. Ohmi merchants, who had started out as mere peddlers and had gone on to achieve resounding success, would provide generous loans to ambitious local youths seeking seed capital and advice to merchants who encountered difficulties. Prosperous merchants would even offer capital to promising members of the younger generation, encouraging them to enter the business of trading. These Ohmi merchants, who established their residences in their hometowns, served as role models for successive generations, and fostered the development of venture-based merchants, thereby creating an inexhaustible supply of future Ohmi merchants.

The elements that served as the foundation for the achievements of the Ohmi merchants, active over time and space for a period exceeding eight hundred years, can be summarized as a fortuitous combination of the blessings of heaven, earth and people. Heaven refers to the region's continuing position as a site of leading developments since ancient times; earth accounts for Ohmi's location, one that fostered both land- and water-based traffic; and people denotes the strong culture of prosperous merchants supporting the rise of future generations. These elements combined to give birth to the emergence of the renowned "merchants from Ohmi."

CHAPTER

1

"Three-Way Satisfaction" and Corporate Social Responsibility (CSR)

The Spirit of *Sanpo-yoshi*—Three-Way Satisfaction

1. Considering a Third-Person Perspective

"Good for the seller, good for the buyer, good for the world"—today, the word *sanpo-yoshi*, or three-way satisfaction is used to symbolize the management philosophy set down by the Ohmi merchants long ago. To achieve three-way satisfaction, a transaction must not only benefit the seller and buyer involved, but must also bring happiness to society as a whole. The renowned Ohmi merchants, who traded throughout Japan, were not satisfied with dealings that simply benefited the seller and buyer, but expanded their view to consider whether it was good for the world. In other words, they considered a third-person perspective, that of the people who lived in the area. In this way, they conducted their business with the utmost care for those around them. The Ohmi merchants were profoundly aware of the fact that they operated their business and conducted transactions as members of society. Through their long history of working as itinerant traders, the Ohmi merchants had learned that success as a business person, and the continued survival and prosperity as a merchant coming from outside, were impossible without the awareness that they were members of society.

2. Born from Ancient Trading Practices

So, what exactly did this itinerant trading of the Ohmi merchants, which gave rise to the philosophy of *sanpo-yoshi*, entail?

The Ohmi merchants did not carry out business in their home province of Ohmi, but rather focused on other provinces, both near and far. They engaged in a manner of trading called *nokogiri-akinai,* or "saw-style trading," in which they would take specialized, finished products such as textiles, sundries and medicinal products (produced around Kyoto and Osaka) to rural regions, and, in turn, bring in the raw materials for those urban products from them. Like a saw, which cuts when being both pushed and pulled, this trade is bi-directional. The Ohmi merchants were truly ahead of their time, managing large-scale businesses that parallel Japan's modern economic and management practices, where raw materials are imported to produce high value-added products using sophisticated technologies for export worldwide.

It was essential for Ohmi merchants, who primarily traded in provinces outside Ohmi, to build the intangible asset of trust with the people in the regions they visited. Itinerant trading was not a business of one-time sales, but instead required the merchant to depart every year to regions and provinces where they sensed success, and develop customers in places where they had neither roots nor relatives to expand their territory.

When Ohmi merchants sought to carry out trade or open stores in other provinces, it was essential for them to earn the trust of the people. The teachings Ohmi merchants preached as essential lessons to succeed in trade outside Ohmi have today been epitomized in the expression *sanpo-yoshi*, a management philosophy born from the ancient trading practices of the Ohmi merchants.

3. The Will of Nakamura Jihei Sogan

The first written document to illustrate the spirit of *sanpo-yoshi* when trading in other provinces was the will written in 1754 by Nakamura Jihei Sogan, a 70-year-old linen trader from Ishibaji village in the district of Kanzaki, left to his fifteen-year-old adoptive heir, Sojiro. The following is a translation of the seven lines that serve as the basis of *sanpo-yoshi*.

Map of Ohmi merchant shops in the Edo Period

Ibaraki
① Yuki
② Shimodate
③ Toride
④ Kasama
⑤ Sakaimachi
⑥ Kurihara
⑦ Kamigo
⑧ Sugama
⑨ Murata
⑩ Hojo
⑪ Kitanagawa
⑫ Koga

Tochigi
⑬ Ashikaga
⑭ Nobushima
⑮ Motegi
⑯ Karasuyama
⑰ Moka
⑱ Oyama
⑲ Chikasono
⑳ Ubagai
㉑ Yatagai
㉒ Yoshino
㉓ Tochigi

Gunma
㉔ Kiryu
㉕ Yabudukahon
㉖ Sakaino
㉗ Tatebayashi
㉘ Ota
㉙ Hino
㉚ Kuragano
㉛ Isesaki
㉜ Itahana
㉝ Fujioka
㉞ Takasaki
㉟ Onishi
㊱ Koizumi

Saitama
㊲ Oshi
㊳ Nagano
㊴ Kumagaya
㊵ Fukaya
㊶ Honjo
㊷ Kodama
㊸ Chichibu
㊹ Shimoyoshida
㊺ Yorii
㊻ Hanno
㊼ Kisai
㊽ Hatogaya
㊾ Omiya

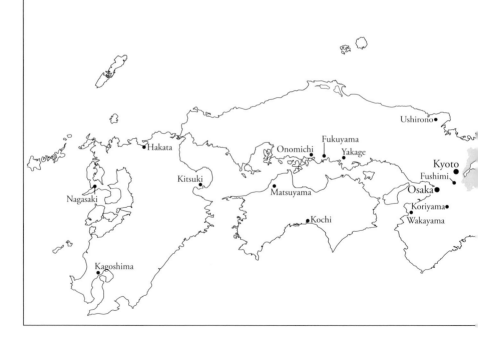

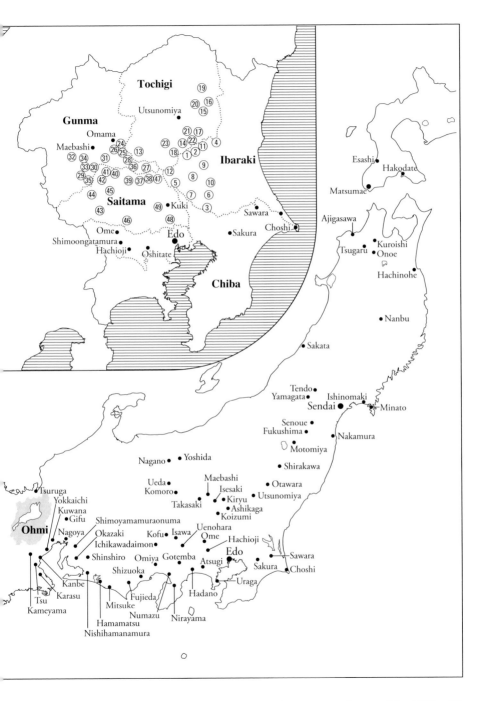

Tochigi

⑲

Utsunomiya ⑳ ⑯
⑮

Gunma

Omama ㉑ ⑰
Maebashi ㉓ ⑭ ㉒ ⑪ ④
㉜ ㉞ ㉛ ㉔ ㉖ ⑬ ⑱ ① ② ④
㉕ ㉘ ㊱ ㉗ Ibaraki
㉝㉚ ㊶㊵ ⑫
㉙㉟ ㊷ ㊴㊲㊳㊷ ⑨
㊺
㊹ ⑤ ⑧ ⑩
Saitama ㊻ ⑦ ⑥
㊸ ⑭㊾ • Kuki ③
㊼ ㊽ Sawara •
Ome • Edo • Sakura Choshi •
Shimoongatamura • Oshitate
Hachioji •

Chiba

Esashi •
Hakodate •
Matsumae •

Ajigasawa •
Tsugaru • Kuroishi •
Onoe •
Hachinohe •

Nanbu •

Sakata •

Tendo •
Yamagata • Ishinomaki
Sendai • Minato
Senoue •
Fukushima •
Nakamura •
Motomiya •
Nagano • Yoshida • Shirakawa •
Ueda • Maebashi • Otawara •
Komoro • Isesaki Utsunomiya •
Takasaki • Kiryu •
Ashikaga •
Koizumi •
Shimoyamamuraonuma Uenohara •
Okazaki Kofu • Isawa Ome
Nagoya Ichikawadaimon Hachioji •
Ohmi Shinshiro • Omiya Gotemba Edo • Sawara •
Tsuruga • Shizuoka Atsugi • Choshi •
Yokkaichi • Sakura •
Kuwana • Uraga •
Gifu • Kanbe Hadano •
Tsu Karasu Fujieda
Kameyama Mitsuke • Numazu Nirayama
Hamamatsu
Nishihamanamura

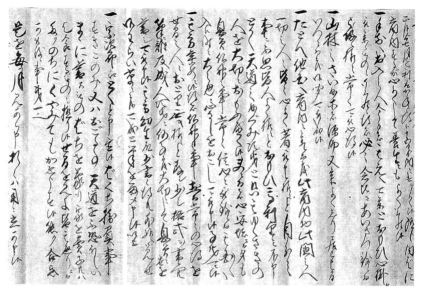

The Will of Nakamura Jihei Sogan

When setting forth to sell your wares in other provinces, let them be a joy to the people there. Every moment pray that your trade serves the people, and trust in the blessings of Heaven for your profits, never deigning to serve yourself through one-time pernicious fees. Hark to strong faith in the gods and buddhas, and be blessed with a sound mind and stout health, all to cherish the people of the lands in which you trade. Remember these things first when entering distant lands, and express them in deeds.

In the first sentence of his will, Sogan uses the abstract expression "the people," to represent all the people, both known and unknown, as well as where they live. Placing absolute priority on bringing satisfaction to people as a whole through the linen and other products they provided is the essential philosophy of a merchant who travels abroad. Sogan explains that ahead of one's own convenience, the utmost consideration must be given to the position of others. To use a modern expression, he is instructing merchants to put customer satisfaction first.

The next section describes the mindset one should hold regarding profit and loss in trading. The phrase "never ... serve yourself through one-time pernicious fees" warns against seeking high one-time profits, and in respect to the ideal level of profits at any time, Sogan advises one to "trust in the blessings of Heaven for your profits."

Linen samples

The closing section recommends having a strong faith in order to suppress one's desire for private gain. In other words, when people go out of their way to trade in places far from their own home, their first desire is often to make a profit. Sogan recommends having strong faith in the *kami* and buddhas to suppress such self-oriented desires.

4. Being a Member of Society

Sogan was not the only Ohmi merchant who emphasized the social nature of commercial behavior. Ono Zensuke I, a devout follower of Jodo Shinshu Buddhism, wrote a "Testament" in 1737, when he was eighty years old. Within the testament, he shared his belief that no matter where people live, if they do not have a heart that cares for others, life will be difficult. He wrote that by always considering the best results for others, staying vigilant against the traps of luxury and pride, and working diligently and with great thrift, he was able to trade throughout the Hokuriku and Tokai regions, and even open a store in Morioka in the far northern reaches of Honshu. A key aspect of the spirit underpinning Ono's philosophy is not only the personal virtues of diligence and frugality backed by strong faith, but the strong emphasis on the spirit of service for the world and society as a whole.

Ono Zensuke I

Furthermore, in his final words before his death in 1854 at the age of seventy-eight, Kobayashi Ginemon I stated that even if you are a simple peddler carrying your wares on a *tenbinbo* shoulder pole (a common practice in Japan at the time, where peddlers carried their wares suspended from both ends of a pole, resting the central portion over their shoulders), if you consider yourself a member of society, avoid being ungrateful and causing trouble to others, and work diligently while caring for the people around you, you will be admired as an upstanding merchant and one day accumulate great assets.

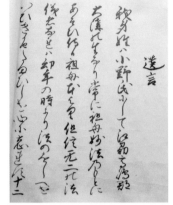
"Testament" of Ono Zensuke I

The Social Consciousness of "Good for the World"

1. A Healthy Tension with Society

The management spirit of the Ohmi merchants, embodied in the phrase "good for the world" within *sanpo-yoshi*, emphasizes, as the foundation of all commercial activities, the importance of social consciousness and serving as a member of society. This remains entirely relevant in our modern era, and companies seeking to be good corporate citizens today can learn a great deal from the philosophy. There is no doubt that companies are organizations founded to seek a profit. However, simply pursuing self-profit without consideration for anything else is only the barest of minimum goals today for any sensible company, and will not inspire employees, nor gain acceptance in society. It is only once all employees feel that the products they offer serve a purpose for their customers and bring them joy, and believe that their business activities are contributing to society, that they can truly feel the significance of working proactively as a member of their company.

In other words, a company must constantly maintain a healthy tension with society, while regularly reflecting on its business activities and staying alert as to whether its activities still have social significance, and whether anyone would be troubled by the absence of the company and its products. This process allows the company to reaffirm its *raison dêtre* on a regular basis. There is an endless list of failures and scandals brought about by companies whose managemant forgot that they are members of society, and pursued only profit for themselves.

2. Relevance to Modern Economics

The spirit of *sanpo-yoshi* can provide two lessons to modern economics and management. Firstly, when considering the issues of modern economics, the issue of the environment is unavoidable. In the modern economic field of resource distribution, sustainable economic growth is a must, which necessitates the securing of resources, while preserving the environment. Overcoming these three challenges remains a major dilemma. The "good for the world" teaching of *sanpo-yoshi* demonstrates the premise that environmental preservation is absolutely essential. This can serve as a hint to solve the dilemma faced by modern economics.

3. Relevance to Modern Management

Sanpo-yoshi also holds a lesson for modern management–its promotion of corporate social contribution by increasing customer satisfaction and fulfilling corporate social responsibility.

The previously mentioned will by Sogan contained teachings for trading in other provinces, such as to refrain from selfishly seeking high interest, entrusting individual profit and loss to the "blessings of Heaven," and devoting oneself only to the thought of serving others. The family precepts of Nishikawa Jingoro in 1807 stated that one should only seek a low margin, never charge an extra margin even if one's stock is low, and never cause any trouble to the society around oneself no matter what. The secret teachings of Tonomura Yozaemon written in 1856 state that the secret of sales lies in always regretting that maybe you had sold at too low of a price. All of these statements can be interpreted as emphasizing that increasing customer satisfaction is the foundation of a sustainable business.

The private Buddhist temple at the former home of Nakamura Jihei

4. Customer Satisfaction

Let us now provide a modern interpretation of these teachings regarding customer satisfaction. The Japanese economy today is defined by deflation, and customers are trending towards lower and lower prices. On the other hand, there is also a trend in which customers do not mind spending a bit extra on valuable products and services that bring them satisfaction or joy. Customers are now diversifying away from seeking only low prices, and are divided into two groups, those who are satisfied by volume, and those who seek products with added quality.

Companies can increase customer satisfaction by capturing these market trends skillfully. There is now demand to create products and services that meet customer needs, and furthermore develop methods of sales and products that uncover needs customers never knew they had.

In the case of apartments, for example, instead of only offering tailor-made apartments, if a company allows customers to alter the room sizes, or the kitchen and bathroom, they can feel the satisfaction of buying an apartment they chose entirely of their own volition, rather than feeling like they were simply sold an existing product.

To take another example from tourism, if a company offers travel plans targeting people of the older generation, who have ample time, stamina, and financial resources, one can help them create precious memories, while developing a base of customers who are likely to come back for a second or third trip.

Whether it is a flower shop, bookstore, liquor store, or any other ordinary, everyday shop, if a business innovates to create satisfaction and value through a unique product lineup that can only be found at its store, it can gain the support of its customers, and develop more regular patrons. Businesses such as these that are built on customer satisfaction can all create more repeat customers and referrals, thus leading to the opening of new, well-developed markets.

5. Contribution to Society

Customer satisfaction is indispensable for the sustainable growth of a store, but if a business wishes to maintain itself as a good member of society, irrespective of the scale at which it operates, it also has the unavoidable duty to fulfill its corporate social responsibility and contribute to society. Indeed, many Ohmi merchants made social contributions to the extent allowed by their resources.

Nakai Shojiemon

While the specifics social contributions are presented in greater detail in the final chapters of this book, a select few examples are provided below. Nakai Shojiemon, who owned a store in Kyoto, personally renovated the Setanokarahashi Bridge in 1815. He also funded the construction of a granite flagstone road for wagons between Kyoto and Otsu, installed impressive 4.5 meter-tall stone lanterns in the post town of Kusatsu on the Tokaido Road, and made many donations to shrines and temples. The donations made by Nakai reached an astonishing total

Setanokarahashi Bridge

of over 8,000 *ryo*. (The *ryo* was a monetary unit used in the Edo period. In today's terms, 1 *ryo* was worth approximately 100,000 yen at the start of the period and approximately 50,000 yen at the end of the period. Nakai lived in the latter, so his donation of 8,000 *ryo* would be equal to approximately US$4 million today).

Other Ohmi merchants also carried out countless anonymous good deeds, such as providing rice and money to the needy during poor harvests, starting

Road paved in granite flagstones   Stone lanterns at Kusatsu Station

An ox-drawn cart traveling the road

construction projects to provide sources of work during famines, paying the annual tax for farmers who could not pay it personally, and allowing people who could not pay back their loans within the agreed period to instead pay back the money when they achieved success in the world, essentially permitting an indefinite period of repayment.

Delivery of annual tributes (*Scenes of Agriculture* Scroll)

6. Social Awareness and Corporate Social Responsibility (CSR)

The term CSR is not prevalent in the West, but has recently caught in Japan as well. It goes without saying that the numerous corporate scandals seen both in Japan and abroad in recent years, and the unmistakable progression of environmental degradation serve as the background to this trend. One could even consider the choice of the World Trade Center in New York as a target for the 9/11 terror attacks as a demonstration of irrational hatred towards globalism. Looking at the practices companies use to maintain a favorable relationship with society, returning a portion of company profits through social contributions used to be enough to achieve a certain level of approval. Going forward, however, the standard of evaluation is likely to shift towards only providing approval to companies that benefit society through their very acts of business. In other words, we will move from seeking social contribution based on results to the fulfillment of social responsibility and social contribution through the business process itself.

After the Japan Association of Corporate Executives, an association of the most preeminent executives in Japan, began advocating CSR as the future foundation of business in March 2003, the Shiga Committee for Economic Development, presented the "Shiga CSR Model" in the spring of 2004, as a method to grasp and improve the current state of management, based on the management philosophy of the Ohmi merchants, embodied in the phrase *sanpo-yoshi*. This presentation is gaining attention as a timely contribution by the very people who carry the DNA of the Ohmi merchants.

The "Corporate Whitepaper" released by the Japan Association of Corporate Executives in April 2013, additionally emphasized that in order to achieve a sustainable management structure and to survive, Japanese corporations must consider and contribute to the wellbeing of their employees and the regions with which they have ties, as members a of global society, in addition to securing profits. The report pointed out that Japanese corporations are lagging behind in globalization efforts despite the increasing severity of global competition, and to achieve success on the world stage going forward, recommended globalizing the "three-way satisfaction" philosophy of the Ohmi merchants, while simultaneously generating continuous innovation and making management decisions in a timely manner. This truly demonstrates that the *sanpo-yoshi* spirit of the Ohmi merchants is a CSR philosophy with deep roots in Japan, and still has value as a global management concept to guide modern business.

A pamphlet explaining CSR by the Japan Association of Corporate Executives

The "Shiga CSR Model" by the Shiga Committee for Economic Development

CHAPTER

2

The Management Practices
of Ohmi Merchants

Diorama of early Ohmi merchants

The Edo Period and the Hometowns of the Ohmi Merchants

1. Society in the Edo Period

The majority of the Ohmi merchants' activities took place in the Edo period, which began in 1603 when Tokugawa Ieyasu placed all of Japan under his control and established his *bakufu* (shogunal government). The shogunate ruled for 265 years, ending in 1867, when the fifteenth shogun, Tokugawa Yoshinobu, returned the right of rule to the emperor. The ruling structure was feudal in nature and composed of the central Edo *bakufu* and individual *han* which were autonomous vassal domains of the shogunate. The term *han* refers both to the domains ruled by daimyo and to the associated system of government. Warriors (samurai) represented the pinnacle of society during the Edo period, with farmers and craftsmen occupying equal status as the rank below. Merchants occupied the lowest rank of the social system. This was because the ruling warrior class, who cherished honor and self-sacrifice, viewed the profits that merchants gained through trade as being the result of self-interest.

2. The Hometowns of the Ohmi Merchants

The Ohmi merchants did not appear out of the blue, nor did they emerge from each part of Ohmi at the same time. In historical order, they first emerged from Takashima, in the district west of the lake, and Hachiman in the Gamo

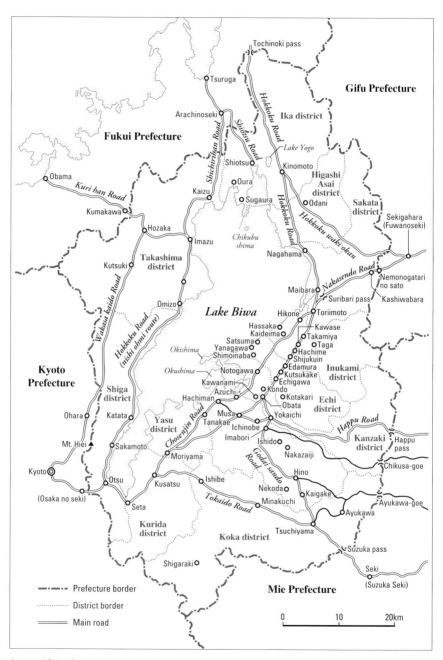

A map of Shiga Prefecture indicating the hometowns and trade routes of the Ohmi merchants

district, and next from Hino, and then Gokasho in the Kanzaki district and the area along the Echigawa River in Echi district. At the end of the Edo period they emerged from Hikone in Inukami district and the Nagahama region in Sakata district. Viewing these regions on the map shows that the Ohmi merchants primarily emerged from specific regions that were situated counterclockwise around Lake Biwa. In other words, the Ohmi merchants originated from areas with a long trading history, namely the area around Lake Biwa where the original Toraijin settlers from the Korean Peninsula had the foresight to open ironworks, and areas that were home to many markets and merchant guilds in the medieval period. In the Warring States period these areas were also early adopters of the *rakuichi-rei* free market edict pioneered by the Rokkaku daimyo, and the new *kokudaka* land valuation system, which estimated the rice production capability of a parcel of land. In the latter half of the Edo period, Ohmi merchants also appeared in the Hikone domain that occupied the eastern and northern regions of Ohmi, where local industrial promotion measures were being implemented at the time.

3. The Hachiman and Takashima Merchants

The merchants of Ohmihachiman on the eastern side of Lake Biwa and the merchants of Takashima on the western shore emerged in the early Edo period, at the time of the *bakufu-han* system. This resulted in the establishment of castle towns all over the country to serve as administrative strongholds, setting off an unprecedented building boom. The majority of modern Japan's regional cities had their genesis at this time. Hachiman merchants such as Nishikawa Jin-

Illustration of the Ohmi merchant shops in Nihonbashi, Edo

goro, Nakamura Kyubei, Ban Denbei, Ban Shoemon, and Yotsugi Kihachiro, quickly opened stores to sell *tatami* reed mats and mosquito nets in Nihonbashi-dori 1-chome, the premier location in Edo, the largest castle town of the day.

A votive picture of a ship donated by Nishimura Taroemon in 1647

The Hachiman and Takashima merchants were also able to establish themselves and prosper as preeminent merchants in the newly founded castle towns of Matsumae in Ezo (modern-day Hokkaido), and Morioka in Mutsu (modern-day Iwate Prefecture), by leveraging the connections they had established through their use of Lake Biwa since the medieval period with the port towns in Obama and Tsuruga on the Sea of Japan coast. Hachiman merchants such as Tazuke Shinsuke, Okada Yazaemon, and Nishikawa Denemon set out to Matsumae, and Takashima merchants such as Ono and Murai established their commercial territory in Morioka. There were even Hachiman merchants who expanded abroad prior to Japan closing its borders, such as Nishimura Taroemon, who travelled to Vietnam, and Shamuroya Kanbei who is said to have traded in Thailand (Siam) during the early part of the seventeenth century when merchant ships (the so-called "red-seal ships") holding letters patent issued by the Tokugawa Shogunate were permitted to trade in Southeast Asia.

4. Hino Merchants

The merchants from the town of Hino made their debut slightly later than the Takashima and Hachiman merchants. As a castle town of the Gamo clan, Hino prospered commercially thanks to the enactment of the *rakuichi-rei* free market edict. The town entered a temporary recession, however,

Toyotomi Hideyoshi

Hino lacquerware bowls

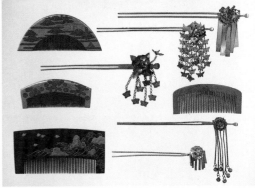

Combs and hairpins

when Toyotomi Hideyoshi (1537–1598), who succeeded Oda Nobunaga and brought all the warring daimyo under his command (and so was called "first within the realm" [*tenkabito*]), transferred Gamo Ujisato (1556–1595) to Matsuzaka in Ise Province. This turned out to be a blessing in disguise. A sense of adversity motivated the local townspeople and, from the latter half of the seventeenth century, merchants began vigorously peddling specialized trade goods such as Hino lacquerware bowls, medical products, *katabira* summer kimonos, and sundry goods. These merchants primarily traded along the Tokaido Road from Kanto region to Kyoto and Osaka. In addition to their sales of

The former residence of Yamanaka Hyoemon

The preservation district in Gokasho Kondo-machi, Higashiohmi City (Photo by author)

silk, cotton and linen kimonos, the merchants established brewery businesses, and would immediately open a store as soon as they had saved 1,000 *ryo*. The many stores opened in this way using small amounts of capital were jokingly called the "1,000 *ryo* shops of Hino."

5. The Koto Merchants

The Koto merchants, primarily centered in Gokasho in Kanzaki district, along the Echigawa River and across Inukami district, began emerging from the start of the eighteenth century. They engaged in itinerant trading of specialized products, such as linen, throughout the country. For example, they obtained silk kimonos and cottonware from the Kyoto and Osaka and Tokaido regions, and sold those products in the Kanto and Tohoku regions. They then purchased products such as Kanto silk kimono textiles, raw silk, and safflower in the Kanto and Tohoku regions, and sold those products in Nagoya, Ohmi, Kyoyo and Osaka and Tango (modern-day northern Kyoto Prefecture). In developing their markets, the Koto merchants avoided the commercial territories of large, established stores, and instead focused on consignment sales to general store merchants on side-roads, and in agricultural and fishing villages. They sold inexpensive products that would meet people's everyday needs. From the early nineteenth century, itinerant trading of linen goods began to thrive in the Chugoku, Shikoku, and Kyushu regions. The activities of the Koto merchants spread throughout Japan, awakening the latent demand among farmers, supported by the normalization of money throughout the population thanks to the monopoly on the sale of specialized goods by the domains.

The Ohmi merchants developed their business outside the province while maintaining their principal residences in Ohmi. They often built homes typ-

The preservation district in Shin-machi, Ohmihachiman City

ical of the prosperous merchants of the time, with the walls of the house covered with old ship's planking and storehouses with white stucco walls. Many of these buildings can still be seen today. The Gokasho Kondo section of Higashiohmi and the Shinmachi area of Ohmihachiman were principal residential districts of the Ohmi merchants and are highly regarded as tourist destinations to see historical townscapes. Both have been designated by the government as Preservation Districts for Groups of Historical Buildings.

SECTION 2
Management Methods and Business Models

1. Itinerant Trading

Peddling was the original business of the Ohmi merchants. They would purchase finished goods in major urban areas, sell them in rural regions, and then purchase local products in the rural areas to sell while returning to their point of origin. This was the so-called *nokogiri-akinai,* or "saw-style trading," a highly efficient form of peddling, and it is no overstatement to say that only merchants who personally succeeded in *nokogiri-akinai* were worthy of being called Ohmi merchants. Itinerant trading served as the foundation of the management systems and business models, each with unique defining characteristics, to be discussed below.

From the start of the Edo period, the Ohmi region produced local goods that could be peddled throughout Japan. Some examples include specialized products such as *tatami* reed mats, mosquito nets, medicinal products and linen. When Ohmi merchants first started peddling, and their funds were low, they would personally carry these specialized products on a simple *tenbinbo* shoulder pole, and set off on round trips to various destinations. On these trips they would travel with relatives and acquaintances from their home region, and gain a foothold in their destination either by obtaining a letter of introduction or through some other means. Once they had become familiar with prominent locals, such as village head, shrine and temple priests and innkeepers, they

Making tatami mats using rush surface mats

Maekawa Zenzaburo in
traveling merchant garb

would send their goods to the destination beforehand by horse or ship, and follow afterwards, carrying only their personal belongings on their iconic *tenbinbo*. At their destination, the merchants would borrow a room at a temple or inn, arrange their goods, and sell them to invited local retail merchants, or carry out negotiations with regional merchants for the sale of consigned goods.

In particular, when consigning their products to retail merchants, Ohmi merchants had to carefully scrutinize both the products for consignment and the merchant who would sell those products. If the Ohmi merchant was not continuously aware of what patterns and colors were popular in the region, and at what prices products sold well, as well as with the character and passion of the retail merchants they would consign their products to, they stood a high chance of losing both their products and their sales revenue. Consigning products to retail merchants required the Ohmi merchants to be highly industrious, regularly visiting the stores of their partner merchants to identify which products were selling well, and to ensure payments were settled properly.

The second generation of the Kobayashi Ginemon merchant house further developed the consignment practices established by the first generation, delivering products when they were requested by their consignment partners instead of unilaterally consigning products to the regional retail merchants. At this stage of development, we can see the merchant house was no longer operating simply as a travelling merchant, but rather as a wholesaler. This wholesaling form of itinerant trading served as the base for the Kobayashi Ginemon house

Traveling merchants

to open a silk, cotton and linen kimono store in Nihonbashi Horidome in Edo in 1831. Before the Tonomura Yozaemon merchant house opened its stores in Kyoto and Osaka, it sold the Joshu linen and silk it procured through travelling sales in the Joshu region (modern-day Gunma Prefecture) to preeminent merchants in Nagoya, such as Shirokiya Tokuemon and Kyoguchiya Kuhachiro.

The key characteristic of the itinerant trading carried out by the Ohmi merchants was their focus on handling a large volume of product through wholesale instead of small volume retail sales. This offered them similarly large opportunities for prosperity.

2. Merchant Unions

As many merchants would set out from Ohmi to peddle throughout Japan, they formed merchant unions to avoid competition at their destinations and to support each other. The traders from Hachiman (modern-day Ohmihachiman) and Satsuma and Yanagawa on the eastern shore of Lake Biwa, who set out for Hokkaido, formed the Ryohama-gumi union in 1737, and worked

The "Ebisu-ko Record Book" from 1764

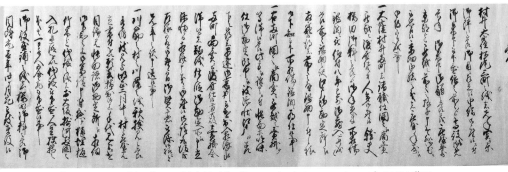

Document recognizing the special right of the Hino merchants to carry out procedures to collect accounts receivable

systematically to negotiate with cargo vessel operators from the Matsumae domain and Hokuriku region to achieve an advantageous position. The merchants from Hachiman, who had stores in Sendai, Mogami, and Fukushima formed the Ebisu-ko union, the peddlers who sold textiles in Wakayama formed the Wakaei-ko union in 1842, the peddlers who traded in Iyo-Matsuyama formed the Sumiyoshi-ko union, and the Ohmi merchants who established themselves in Kyushu formed the Eiku-ko union.

The largest of all these merchant unions was the Hino-daitoban-nakama union formed by the Hino merchants. The town of Hino was divided into six groups, and these groups took annual turns administering the union. It was officially established in 1690, the same year it formulated its bylaws,

A sign hung outside a special lodge for Hino merchants

and it continued its activities until the end of the nineteenth century. Central to the union were the privileges accorded by the *bakufu* enabling it to carry out litigation related to accounts receivable and loans, and a system through which merchants could freely use designated lodgings along the Tokaido and Nakasendo Roads. Thus the Hino-daitoban-nakama union secured the benefit of simple procedures to perform litigation for the payment of sales proceeds generated in the itinerant trading it carried out over a vast area, together with the convenience of being able to use the designated lodging system on its sales trips.

3. Regional Product Rotation

Once Ohmi merchants built up their funds through itinerant trading, they would open multiple stores in strategic locations regardless of the distance. These stores would serve as their most advanced bases to deliver and store goods, allowing the merchants to further extend their reach from these branches with "leaf" stores.

Once they opened stores in both eastern and western Japan, the merchants could rotate the goods from different regions between their various stores. They would use the information network they established between their stores to adjust the supply and demand of goods, and this inter-regional product rotation that targeted the price differences between regions was a form of large-scale itinerant trading known as *shokoku-sanbutsu-mawashi*, or "regional product rotation." The creativity to sense the enormous business opportunity regional product rotation presented, and the capability to turn that opportunity into reality, were likely one of the factors that led to the wealth of the Ohmi merchants.

The products produced in the Kyoto and Osaka regions distributed by the Ohmi merchants throughout Japan using both land and sea routes, were known as *kudashini*, or goods "sent down" from the center. These were primarily products produced in urban regions such as sundries (combs, hairpins, white facial powder, stationery, etc.), mosquito nets, medicinal products, *tatami* mats, linen, cotton, and kimonos. The Ohmi merchants did not only buy and sell these products, but also involved themselves in the production of sundries, medicines and linen textiles.

The goods and materials Ohmi merchants procured in the rural regions to trade in urban areas were known as *noboseni*, or goods "sent up." The active assistance of the Ohmi merchants in introducing new technologies and opening up markets brought prosperity to the fishing industry of Hokkaido, and helped develop raw materials such as the raw silk, Kanto kimono, linen, and safflower of the Kanto and Tohoku regions and to commercialize them.

Here we will illustrate a few key examples of regional product rotation. The Nakai Genzaemon merchant house held a network of over twenty stores spanning the Tohoku region in northern Japan to Kyushu in the south. It carried out regional product rotation between its Tohoku stores and those in urban areas. The most popular product the Nakai delivered to their Tohoku branches from the urban areas was used clothing (*furute*). Urban dwellers in places such as Kyoto were known far and wide for their extravagance in clothing, to the point it was said that the people of Kyoto

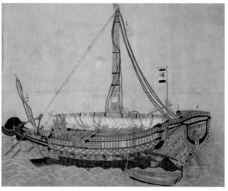

A *higaki* sailing freight ship

are bankrupted by clothing. There was an enormous demand, on a scale that can hardly be imagined today, in the Tohoku region for this used clothing, for everything from formal, luxurious clothing to everyday work clothes.

The Nakai house collected used urban clothing at its Fushimi and Osaka stores and sent it to the Tohoku region together with ginned cotton picked from the seed, medicinal seeds, and oil. These "sent down" goods would be shipped to Edo or Uraga (in modern-day Kanagawa Prefecture) using cargo ships called *higaki*. Some of these products would be unloaded and sold in Edo, and the remainder would be shipped on, together with used clothing from Edo, to the Sendai branch of the Nakai house using both land and sea routes. The products would then be sold wholesale to stores in the Tohoku region from the Sendai branch.

At its regional branch stores in Sendai and Otawara, the Nakai house would collect products such as raw silk, ramie fiber, safflower, wax, soybeans, kidney beans, lacquer, and silkworms from the Kanto and Tohoku regions. These "sent up" goods would then be shipped via sea and land routes primarily to the Osaka store of the Nakai house, and resold through its network of stores in urban areas. Nakai Genzaemon I used this method of regional product rotation to increase his net assets from 7,468 *ryo* in 1769 to 87,255 *ryo* in 1796, a growth of over 1,000 percent.

The Nakai house was not the only group of Ohmi merchants to engage in regional product rotation. From the start of the Edo period, the Hachiman merchants, together with merchants from the neighboring regions of Satsuma and Yanagawa, established themselves in Matsumae, Hokkaido. They delivered rice, miso, salt, and used clothing to the island, and carried back marine products such as herring, salmon, fish roe and kombu seaweed on the return trip to Kyoto and Osaka. A portion of these marine products produced in Hokkaido were delivered to Nagasaki in the southern island of Kyushu to be exported to

Aquatic products from Hokkido's fishing industry

Qing China. To facilitate the marine transport of freight cargo between Hokkaido and other regions, the Ohmi merchants organized the ships of Hashidate in Kaga Province (modern-day Ishikawa Prefecture), and the Kono and Tsuruga areas in Echizen Province (modern-day Fukui Prefecture), into dedicated chartered cargo ships known as *nidokobune*.

The Ono and Murai merchant union of Omizo District in the district of Takashima opened a number of stores in Kyoto and in the northern town of Morioka. The union would gather "sent up" goods from the rural Morioka region such as gromwell root, safflower, raw silk, ramie fiber, lacquer and wax. These goods would then be shipped to Kyoto and other urban regions. "Sent down" goods such as ginned cotton, cotton, used clothing, sundries, candles, sugar and porcelain would then be shipped from the urban regions to Morioka. The union established what was virtually a relationship of raw materials and finished products between the two regions, producing large profits.

The trading practice of regional product rotation can be considered a true prototype of the business model of modern trading companies. This trading practice, which met the demands of both urban and rural regions, was not only a source of great wealth for the Ohmi merchants, but also served to disseminate culture to rural areas through the delivery of urban products, and to stimulate regional industries there.

4. Organizational Accounting

The merchant house accounting ledger represents the peak achievement of rational management. As part of its accounting process, starting in 1746, the Nakai house created an annual financial statement for each branch using that branch's *daifukucho* (central general ledger). This ledger recorded the transactions made every day in chronological order, without any categorization. It consisted of half-sheets of paper bound together horizontally to form a thick book. In a calculation similar to today's balance sheet accounting, they subtracted their start-of-year assets and any debt assumed in the accounting year from their assets held at the end of the year. To calculate their profit and loss statement, they then subtracted their annual expenses from their annual revenue, and reconciled the resulting number against the balance sheet.

In the same period, the Tonomura Yozaemon house and the Yao Kihei house also performed their accounting according to the same principle of double entry. Though slightly later than others, the Nishikawa Jingoro house also adopted an orderly system of double-entry accounting in 1807. Furthermore, the Ono Zensuke house of the Kosei region also carried out double-entry style accounting. Many Ohmi merchants from Hino similarly prepared financial statements for their stores according to the principle of double-entry accounting, such as the Shimazaki Zenbei house, the Shimazaki Rihei house, the Oka Chubei house, the Yano Shinemon house, the Yano Kyuzaemon house, the Kaido Kaemon house, and the Okazaki Denzaemon house.

The Ohmi merchants were required to adopt a systematic method of bookkeeping to manage the transaction-related

Daifukucho

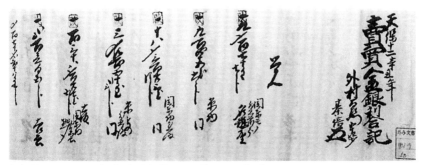

A double-entry accounting book of the Tonomura Yozaemon family

information at their network of branch and leaf stores, and this high level of rationality met the same standards achieved by the double-entry accounting carried out in the West during the same period. It is not yet known, however, how the techniques of double-entry accounting were shared between the Ohmi merchants. A deeply interesting topic of continuing investigation is whether a systemized Ohmi double-entry bookkeeping method existed.

5. Branch Stores, Leaf Stores and *Noriai-akinai* Joint Ventures

The commercial territory of the Ohmi merchants in the Edo period ranged from Kagoshima in the south to Hokkaido in the north, and the merchants established numerous stores between the two points. Products were shipped over land and sea to reap enormous profits, and the Ohmi merchants operated at a scale that far surpassed that of the merchants of other regions. The Ohmi merchants based themselves at their primary residences in Ohmi, and referred to the smaller stores they opened around their branch stores as "leaf" stores. They opened these branch and leaf stores wherever they sensed opportunity, keen never to miss a chance for commercial success.

The Ohmi merchants would open stores according to the old phrase, "Three *ri* (12 kilometers) in all directions, open a store wherever they eat rice from the pot." This referred to their practice of establishing stores in affluent regions where the people were wealthy enough to eat rice regularly and where there would likely be robust purchasing power. The Ohmi merchants would then use these stores as bases while expanding their territory further into key regions with branch and leaf stores.

Examining the distribution of branch and leaf stores in the Edo period (as illustrated on the map on page 26, 27), one can see stores located throughout nearly all of Japan, centered on Edo, Kyoto and Osaka. East of the Kyoto and Osaka regions however, particularly eastern Kanto and through the Tohoku region, there was a strikingly dense distribution of stores. The reason for this is that western Japan was home to many powerful lords, who often controlled entire provinces, and the regulations were correspondingly strict in their territories. Furthermore, the natural conditions were largely the same as those of the central urban regions. The opening of a store in the west was therefore not very attractive. Eastern Japan, on the other hand, was home to many minor lords, and saw accordingly loose regulations, which made it easy for merchants from other parts of the country to enter the territory. The natural and economic conditions were also very different from those of the central urban regions, offering the chance for considerable commercial profit simply by opening a store.

Opening a network of branch stores, carrying out regional product rotation sales throughout that network, producing specialized goods, and expanding new businesses such as brewing all required the preparation of a significant amount of business capital. The Ohmi merchants created the *noriai-akinai* (business association) system of incorporation to serve as a joint venture investment system to facilitate the capital procurement required to establish networks of stores.

For example, the Sendai branch of the Nakai Genzaemon merchant house was initially opened in the form of a joint investment in 1769. The joint venture was divided into 20 shares, which were purchased by the joint investors, all relatives and acquaintances of the Nakai, according to the following amounts: the first generation Genzaemon (3,357 *ryo*, 13.50 shares), Yano Shinemon (500 *ryo*, 2.00 shares), Ida Sukeemon (500 *ryo*, 2.00 shares), Sugii Kyuemon (312 *ryo* 2 *bu*, 1.25 shares), Wakimura Sobei (312 *ryo* 2 *bu*, 1.25 shares). The investors assumed unlimited liability, received interest payments according to their investments, and shared profits according to the number of shares they held.

The Sendai branch, however, met with many disasters, such as the famines of the Tenmei era in the 1780s, and the invalidation of the Sendai *hansatsu* currency (unexchangeable paper currencies that could only be used in a specific domain, issued by a *han* government facing financial difficulties). Thus, all the investors except Genzaemon withdrew their investments, leaving the Sendai branch to be solely managed by the Nakai house.

The Yao Kihei merchant house, which in 1749 had established a brewery business and sundry branch stores in the Chichibu area of Musashi Province (modern-day Saitama Prefecture), also opened stores in the Kanto region through a *noriai-akinai* joint venture. Of the sixteen stores opened by the Yao house, nine were breweries. In its network of branch stores built around breweries, the Yao house would take over the brewing licenses, breweries, sake delivery tools and stores as going concerns from prominent local individuals who held sake brewing licenses, and send its own employees to run the businesses as managers.

This method of business made it possible to enter the sake brewing business with a small amount of capital, despite it normally requiring enormous fixed capital investment. Executing this business model in a *noriai-akinai* joint venture with a partner who was actively seeking capital made it possible to open stores with even smaller amounts of capital.

Other examples of *noriai-akinai* joint ventures include the organization formed by the Hachiman merchant Nishikawa Denji to deliver goods from Matsumae domain in Hokkaido to Nagasaki; the official trading monopoly on Etorofu island in Hokkaido acquired by Fujino Shirobei, Nishikawa Denemon and Okada Yazaemon; and the Inanishi Kimono Wholesale Store founded in Osaka by Inamoto Riemon and Nishimura Jurobei through an equal investment by both parties.

Managing multiple stores through *noriai-akinai* joint ventures allowed participants

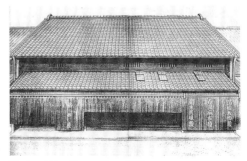

The Inanishiya Kimono Shop, 1864

to spread the capital, regional, and business-sector risks they faced while also assigning the very best personnel. Diversifying one's investments allowed precious capital to be invested more effectively. Distribution through a network of stores across many regions reduced the exposure to large, one-time losses caused by a failed harvest in a particular area. Participants would also involve themselves in a range of industries, from fishing to manufacturing and finance, to achieve business-sector diversification. From the perspective of human resource management, *noriai-akinai* joint ventures allowed the most skilled employees to be sent to key stores as managers, thus making the most of their abilities.

It is clear that the Ohmi merchants were motivated to open stores through *noriai-akinai* joint ventures based on principles of rational management. The joint venture system allowed them to expand their business with a smaller investment of personal capital, or distribute the capital risk posed by the venture, and additionally assign the very best employees to the new business.

6. The *Zaisho-nobori* Homecoming System

Two paths were available to individuals hoping to become Ohmi merchants. The first option was to immediately start as an independent peddler, and the second option was to join an existing major merchant house as a type of apprentice (*hokonin*) and then establish their own merchant house afterwards, their final goal. Such employees would be recognized for their service to the merchant house and permitted by its head to establish their own independent house (*bekke*). Training and employee development was an important aspect of the second option.

Ohmi merchants employed the *zaisho-nobori* "homecoming" system to manage employees. Here, the number of times

Hokonin-ukejo

an employee returned home to Ohmi from a remote store was linked to their promotion at the store to which they were assigned. All the Ohmi merchants adhered to the practice of only assigning men from Ohmi to their stores in strategic regions. Everyone at the branch store would live together communally, from its head down through the various ranks of senior manager (*shihainin*), manager (*banto*) and clerk (*tedai*), to the lowest ranked employees, who were youths known as *detchi* (apprentice). Having employees with well-recognized backgrounds and shared customs fostered a strong sense of team spirit, and formed a robust foundation that supported the businesses of the Ohmi merchants. From that perspective, one could consider the employees at the branch stores of Ohmi merchants as their standing army in the great war of commerce.

A school-based education system had yet to be established in the Edo period, and young men seeking to join a store at about the age of twelve would rely on local acquaintances or relatives to find a guarantor to help make their application. If they were considered to be promising candidates, an employee at the store would submit a *hokonin-ukejo* to the shop's master. This was a document that served as both a contract of employment and a certificate of guarantee for the employee, with details such as the new employee's name, date of birth, age, parents, sectarian affiliation, and the name of their guarantor. The conditions of employment were also recorded, and the new employee was required to adhere to all of the stipulations in the *hokonin-ukejo*.

If the applicant was accepted as an employee, he would first receive training in manners by the wife of the head of the merchant house at his home, and only once he passed a trial period lasting several months would he be accepted as a full employee. She would carefully scrutinize the candidate's character and capabilities, and he would be dispatched to a store that

Detchi servants traveling to work in Edo

best matched his characteristics. At the store, the employee would be given a new name for use in the store, and start life there at the lowest rank of *detchi*, carrying out odd-jobs at the store. Following his coming of age ceremony (*genpuku-shiki*) at the age of 15 or 16 he would be permitted to take his first trip home in five years to see his parents in Ohmi. This was called *hatsu-nobori*. After returning to the store, the employee would be promoted to the next rank of clerk (*tedai*), and take on a role in sales and other areas. After working for another three years, he was permitted to take a second trip home (called *naka-nobori*), after which he would be again promoted. Once he achieved the rank of *banto* (manager) or *shihainin* (senior manager) he would be allowed to return home for approximately fifty days every year, typically making it possible to get married at about the age of thirty-five, when he would become independent and establish his own merchant house. He would then have spent over twenty years as a live-in employee at the store he had first joined.

Because the Ohmi merchants opened branch stores in regions far away from their hometowns, their employees could not return home on the *yabuiri* days of rest (January and July 15–16 of every year) like the employees of other merchant houses. Because of this, the Ohmi merchants implemented the *nobori* system allowing employees approximately fifty days, including travel time, at home every few years.

Such visits home served as demarcations within their long tenure at their store, and in addition to serving as a period of relaxation, it was also a time for the employee's performance to be evaluated. Employees who performed well could return to their stores, but those who were not fit to be merchants were dismissed. This means that the more times an employee returned, the greater his promotion. In this sense, the *zaisho-nobori* system was a system based on merit rather than seniority, with personnel selection based on a strict appraisal of performance.

CHAPTER

3

Life History of the Entrepreneur Ito Chubei

Ito Chubei I

Itinerant Trading

1. The Beginnings of General Trading Companies

Ito Chubei I is the founder of two modern day general trading companies (*sogo shosha*): the Itochu Corporation and the Marubeni Corporation. *Sogo shosha* is a form of general trading company unique to Japan. Mitsubishi Corporation, Mitsui & Co., Itochu Corporation, Sumitomo Corporation, and Marubeni Corporation are considered the five major trading companies of Japan, and are also some of the largest trading companies to operate globally. *Sogo shosha* are global companies that operate in a wide range of fields, including textiles, machinery, metals, energy, food, chemicals, logistics, finance, and data. In recent years, both Itochu Corporation and Marubeni have achieved annual revenues exceeding five trillion yen.

Chubei I was born on August 7, 1842, the second son of Ito Chobei from Hachime Village in the district of Inukami on the eastern shore of Lake Biwa. The Ito family was a local merchant family that operated only within the Ohmi region, selling silk, cotton and linen kimonos to retail customers. Chubei's elder brother, Chobei, took over the family business. As the second son, Chubei was encouraged by

The former residence of Ito Chubei (Photo by author)

his father to establish his own, independent trading house.

In 1858, at the age of seventeen, Chubei borrowed 50 *ryo* of seed capital from his uncle, and, under his guidance, began itinerant trading of Ohmi's linen textiles in Kyoto, Osaka and Wakayama.

2. Expanding to Kyushu

In 1853, Commodore Matthew C. Perry (1794–1858) led the East Indian Squadron of the United States Navy to Japan, bearing a sovereign message from President Millard Fillmore. He entered Edo Bay at the head of a formation of four battleships aboard his state-of-the-art flagship, the 2,450-ton USS *Susquehanna*, which bore a total of seventy cannons. This act sparked the eventual collapse of the Edo shogunate, and the fifteen years of domestic turmoil that accompanied the founding of the Meiji government. The Edo shogunate was no longer able to maintain the isolation of Japan that had lasted for over two hundred years, and opened up the country to free trade with the West in 1859.

That same year, Chubei had just started branching out to Kyushu and extended himself to Nagasaki. Kyushu is one of the four main islands of Japan, and is located in the southwest region of the archipelago, approximately 800 kilometers from Ohmi. In Nagasaki, Chubei was able to witness first-hand the true nature of overseas trade, seeing the "black ships" of the West, and foreign people and trading houses. In his later years, he recounted this time as a wonderful, eye-opening experience. The knowledge Chubei gained was also the inspiration for his later founding of the Itochu and Marubeni *sogo shosha* general trading companies. In 1861, Chubei hired local *uriko* salespeople to whom he could consign his products, and *tedai* sales clerks to assist him in transporting

Commodore Perry and his flagship

his goods to northern Kyushu, in order to begin selling linen and *minojima* textiles (cotton and mixed weave silk floss textiles produced in the Hashima region of modern-day Gifu Prefecture).

However, the Ohmi merchants who preceded Chubei had already formed the exclusive Eiku-ko trade association, which sought to prevent new Ohmi merchants from entering the market. To overcome this obstacle, Chubei held a meeting in a small warehouse in northern Kyushu, facing the thirteen-member council of the Eiku-ko association. He entered into vigorous debate with the council and succeeded in winning them over through his powers of persuasion. He was even nominated to become head of the association the following year.

To deliver linen to Kyushu from his hometown of Hachime, Chubei first had to transport it from his home to Lake Biwa, four kilometers to the west. It would then be loaded onto a ship and sailed to the port of Otsu, where it was unloaded and carried over the mountains by oxen wagons to Kyoto. In Kyoto, the linen was transferred to *takase-bune* ferries which navigated the city's canals to Fushimi on the banks of the Yodo River. From Fushimi, *sanjik-koku-bune* river barges would carry the linen to Osaka, where the goods were divided, and finally taken across the Seto Inland Sea to Kyushu on sea-going vessels. Chubei worked tirelessly through all stages of the process together with his clerks and porters. He had discerned Kyushu to be a preeminent commercial region, and was determined to set down roots in northern Kyushu, centered on Hakata, which now forms the central part of the modern city of Fukuoka.

3. Joint Sales with His Brother and Liquidation

Meanwhile, the family business, which had been taken over by Chubei's elder brother, Chobei, was not doing well. By 1864, the assets held by Chubei already exceeded those of his elder brother, and at Chobei's request, the brothers combined their assets and divided their profits. In 1867, Chobei stopped selling locally in Ohmi and joined Chubei in the itinerant trading he had established. The two brothers thus began joint trading activities. In their settlement of accounts for 1870 Chobei had accumulated assets of 10,400 *ryo* and Chubei 7,200 *ryo*. In the same year, at Chobei's request, the two divided their shared commercial territory, and began managing their businesses independently.

In the agreement that was put down in writing between the two brothers, the assets of the *honke* (main house) of Chobei, the elder, and the *bunke* (branch house) of Chubei, the younger, would be entirely separated. The preamble of the agreement stated that even after the division of assets, the two brothers should continue helping each other and maintain friendly relations in life. Next, in order to prevent a gap in assets from appearing between the two brothers due to the vagaries of fate, it was stated that each brother should help the other by transferring up to twenty percent of their profits after their annual accounting. The agreement was made for a term of ten years. In the division of the commercial territory, the *honke* was granted an advantageous territory comprised of Shimonoseki, a key port city facing the Kanmon Straits between the western edge of Honshu and the eastern edge of Kyushu, and the whole of Kyushu. The *bunke* was granted the territory leading up to Shimonoseki, a narrow region that was little known to Chubei.

The revolutionary policies rapidly enacted by the new Meiji government caused upheaval in the economy of Japan. Chubei was unable to achieve success in his new territory and was pessimistic about his prospects in the region. He bravely decided to abandon the new territory he was granted through his agreement with Chobei. In January 1872, the year following their agreement,

The division of commercial territories between the Ito brothers in 1870, "Sadame"

Chubei sought to renegotiate his territory with Chobei, requesting that his brother relinquish the port city of Shimonoseki. Chobei declined to return Shimonoseki and instead recommended that Chubei open a store in Osaka. The negotiations concluded with Chubei accepting Chobei's suggestion. Immediately after the

Illustration of the Ito-mise shop of Ito Chubei

negotiations concluded, Chubei handed over his entire business to Chobei, and began his journey home to Ohmi. He stopped over in Osaka to scout for a prime location to open a store, before returning to Ohmi on February 8, 1872.

SECTION 2

Innovative Management

1. Opening a Store in Osaka

On February 13, 1872, at the age of 31, Chubei rented a residence in the Honmachi 2-chome neighborhood of Senba, the business center of Osaka, and opened his own independent silk, cotton and linen kimono wholesale store, Ito Chubei Shoten, using the trade name "Benchu." In 1875, Chubei established his store rules and opened a new store in the Honmachi 3-chome neighborhood. By this time, he had hired seven employees.

When Chubei opened his store in Osaka, the *kabunakama* trade cartel system of the merchant guilds that had been in place since the Edo period was already on the decline, and when it was finally banned, the entry of new merchants to Osaka was greatly eased. This created a rush of Ohmi merchant groups trying to expand into Osaka. Chubei's decision to follow the advice of his often-unreasonable older brother, boldly giving up the commercial territory he had personally toiled to establish and opening a store in Osaka, not only demonstrated his dutiful character and deep fidelity to the principle of respecting one's elders, but also revealed the depth of his discernment in foreseeing the limits of Japan's itinerant trade given the advent of free trade with foreign countries. Chubei's insightful, timely decision opened the path for him to found major trading companies still known today.

2. Thriving Business

Business at Chubei's Osaka store grew steadily. In 1884 he opened a store in Kyoto selling Kyoto kimonos, and in 1893 he opened the Ito Thread and Yarn Store. This would later be split to become Itochu and Marubeni. In his trading business, Chubei opened a felt and woolen textile store in 1886, and dispatched employees to Britain and Germany to begin importing goods. From around 1890, Chubei began directly exporting sundry goods to the United States and in 1896 founded a limited partnership company called Nitto to carry out trade with China, dealing in raw cotton wool and cotton yarn. During this period, Chubei was involved in the founding of ten firms, including the Ohmi Bank, and in other businesses such as warehousing and insurance. At the time of his death at the age of sixty-two in 1903, 100 people were employed across his thriving business enterprises.

3. Selecting and Caring for Employees

Chubei was active at a time of great upheaval in Japan, with the collapse of the Edo shogunate, followed shortly by the establishment of the new Meiji government. Just to achieve healthy business growth, Chubei had to engage in innovative management practices. The symbol of these was his decisive selection of young employees. He appointed a young man in his twenties to serve as the senior manager of his flagship store Benchu, and the senior manager of his Kyoto store was also only twenty years of age. Chubei assigned procurement duties to a young sixteen-year-old, who had only joined his store four years earlier, and promoted an eighteen-year-old, who had only just joined his enterprise, to the prestigious position of manager of his Ito Thread and Yarn Store.

In his trading businesses as well, Chubei, a prominent store head around the age of fifty, worked alongside young staff members in their twenties. The youth of Chubei's employees stood out compared to other stores in the same industry. By entrusting his young employees with both freedom and authority, while also clearly laying out their responsibilities, Chubei was able to stimulate their enthusiasm and initiative.

In addition to boldly selecting young people as employees, Chubei was also attentive to their treatment. For example, immediately after opening his Osaka store, Chubei provided beef to the employees who lived there. At first, he provided employees working the long night shift with *sukiyaki*, a beef dish, as a form of late night comfort food. On the first and fifteenth of every month, he would prepare a celebratory feast with a whole sea bream for his employees, ordering it from a *shidashiya* caterer to be served as the store's regular meal. When concerns about fire stopped *sukiyaki* being served on the night shift, Chubei turned around and served it six times a month on dates containing a one or six starting from around 1885. He attended these meals in person and employees mingled in an atmosphere free from hierarchy and strict manners, with sake flowing freely to help them deepen their relationships. Looking at the typical meals of other merchant stores at the time, which offered extremely simple fare containing hardly any meat and served salted sardines twice a month as the primary source of protein, it is clear that Chubei set himself apart with his treatment of his employees. He abandoned deeply-rooted feudal customs that remained at the time, where it was a matter of course for the run of employees to be treated outrageously, and handled his employees with the same loving care one would offer a child.

Similar to other Ohmi stores, Chubei's employees were primarily from the Ohmi region, and they frequently returned there from Osaka. Regulations were established for travel expenses to be provided to return home, and all ranks, from store head to apprentice, received the same treatment. This equal treatment was another example of Chubei's deep love for his employees.

Chubei was strongly convinced that he was entrusted with the social mission to develop his employees so that they could one day achieve independence. As stated previously, he boldly granted his employees discretionary rights and opportunities for training based on his heartfelt belief that his employees were partners in business rather than simple servants. Chubei also strictly forbade his employees from giving him mid-summer and year-end gifts, as would have been customary at other stores.

At the same time as holding deep affection for his employees, whom he had trained from the age of twelve, Chubei was also equally exacting. With fire in his eyes, he instructed or corrected his employees with unreserved strictness. He unfailingly reprimanded employees by name, and would point out the various points that needed to be corrected or improved upon. Even the boldest employees were said to be struck entirely motionless when they were upbraided by Chubei. When he was visiting one of his stores, the atmosphere was one of strict solemnity. Memorials left behind by his various employees paint pictures of a tense and quiet atmosphere whenever Chubei was present, one far different from the everyday mood, so much so that a young clerk returning to the store from running errands would surely immediately and instinctively sense that his master was present. Whenever Chubei was around, an air of dignified gravitas would permeate the store.

4. Meeting System

Chubei developed his employees by improving their proficiency and competence through a meeting system. He first began holding meetings when he opened his Osaka store in 1872. Within these meetings, the general direction of the store's management would be decided through public consensus among the employees. The system of meetings was codified in 1885, establishing regular monthly meetings, semiannual grand meetings, and exceptional meetings as needed. Chubei personally served as the chairman of the semiannual grand meetings, and the individual store heads would serve as the chairmen of the regular monthly meetings. At the semiannual grand meetings, the primary topics were an assessment of the business' commercial policy, and resolutions on business and human resource-related matters such as points for improvement, supervision, and roles and responsibilities. Employees who had established themselves as veterans were permitted to attend the grand meetings. At the regular monthly meetings, a wide range of topics related to store management and the industry would be freely discussed by employees of all ranks, such as the economy, market prices, procurement, stock levels, and the appropriateness of product prices. Resolutions were reached on major topics based on discussion and voting, and even young employees were permitted to attend the meetings.

New employees were particularly prone to being strictly admonished at the meetings, which required them to constantly prepare for the meetings in their daily activities, and always hold an attitude of self-improvement. Being permitted to attend the meetings was a great ambition and honor for young employees, but together with instilling affection and camaraderie among attendees, the meetings also fostered an atmosphere of rigorous competition between the various attendees. Employees who did not commit themselves to diligence and self-improvement in their everyday duties were forced to refrain from attending the meetings.

All employees, including Chubei himself, were bound by the resolutions of the meetings, and the system of meetings therefore served as a source of great motivation for Chubei's employees. The various meetings, which guaranteed employees equal rights to speak, also served as opportunities to establish management policy based on shared understanding and consensus, and to forge the next generation of leaders.

Chubei's system of meetings, which could be considered democratic in nature, was highly progressive for his time, and was founded on his innovative ideas regarding freedom and autonomy.

To understand Chubei's perspective on freedom, we can examine the words Chubei II attributed to his father, "*Gekokujo* (subordinates winning the debate against superiors) is the best way to expand your ideas." It goes without saying that freedom of expression is a prerequisite to a debate between inferiors and superiors. It is also said that Chubei was fond of teaching his employees that, "prosperity can be found where people have true freedom." Chubei's words resonated deeply with those of Fukuzawa Yukichi (1835–

1901), the founder of Keio University and a progressive opinion leader of his day, who advocated self-reliance and dignity, which meant conducting one's affairs independently, and maintaining one's character and dignity. Chubei was convinced that freedom was an indispensable element in the growth of both his employees and his business.

Fukuzawa Yukichi

5. Dividing Profits Three Ways

Chubei's belief in sharing prosperity with his employees can also be seen in his treatment of profits. His financial management system was based on the *mitsuwari-seido* system of dividing profits three ways, which had been practiced by Ohmi merchants since the Edo period. Dividing the net profit into three parts was one of the founding rules Chubei established when he opened his Osaka store. Profits were divided into the Ito house profits, savings for his flagship Osaka store, and for distribution among his employees. Chubei revised this rule in 1893 because of the expansion of his business, and changed the portions, allocating fifty percent of the net profit to the Ito family, thirty percent as savings for the flagship Osaka store, and the remaining twenty percent for distribution among employees. Of the twenty percent of profits allocated to employees, two thirds was distributed as annual salary, and the remaining one third retained by the Ito family to pay merit bonuses.

In this way, when employees advanced through all the ranks, including that of senior manager, and were thus ready to establish their own independent merchant house (*bekke*), Chubei would pay the bonus as a single large sum to serve as seed money for the employee's venture. Chubei's highly progressive policy of sharing his profits with his employees was based on his strong belief in developing those who worked for him. When explaining his business philosophy to those close to him, Chubei stated that, "Rather than raising one son, I'd like to raise one hundred new merchant houses. That is the true road to commercial success. First and foremost, rather than profits, I want to first of all provide happiness to my employees." These words clearly show that realizing happiness among his employees was the first priority in Chubei's business philosophy.

6. Love for Osaka and Enmity for Kyoto

While the opening of his Osaka store in 1872 was a once in a lifetime personal challenge for Chubei, it was also one part of the general trend of the time, a period when countless groups of Ohmi merchants set out to expand their business into Osaka. Chubei, who naturally spoke the dialect of his native town in Ohmi his entire life and preferred to approach matters in a decisive way, easily adapted to the egalitarian, frank and fast-paced culture of Osaka.

Osaka was a castle town that had developed during the Edo period by people who gathered from the surrounding regions of Hirano, Sakai, Joshuyawata, Fushimi and Ohmi. It was a place where people did not make much of another person's pedigree or background. Although it was a so-called "castle town," Osaka Castle was actually located on the outskirts of the actual city, which centered on the merchant townhouses in Senba, making it an easygoing place where residents could get by without even knowing the names of the shogunal officials who governed the city and were replaced every few years.

Chubei felt, by contrast, great enmity for Kyoto. As a city with long traditions that developed around the Imperial Palace, its residents paid great attention to family pedigree and time-honored stores, carefully separating their true feelings from what they said in public, and were highly wary of

Osaka Castle

Kyoto Imperial Palace

outsiders. Chubei's direct and decisive character was at odds with all of these characteristics. While Chubei opened a Kyoto store in recognition of the city's many impeccable crafts that could be found nowhere else, it was a place where he never felt at home.

Osaka was an open-minded city that was much more welcoming than Kyoto to a newcomer like Chubei. In return, Chubei expressed great love for the city that suited him temperamentally and offered him such an easy place to work, and together with his employees, Chubei enjoyed its many seasonal pleasures such as riverside terraces, night markets, flower and garden markets, and the Ebisu Festival of January 10.

7. Chubei's Wife, Yae

Looking back at the relationship between Chubei and his wife, Yae, provides a typical example of marital relations and the role women played in the world of the Ohmi merchants that existed through to World War II.

Yae was born in 1849, and in 1866, at the age of eighteen, she married Chubei, who was twenty\five years old at the time. Yae and Chubei had two sons and two daughters, but their first son died at a young age. Yae's second son, Seiichi, would go on to inherit the name of Chubei II. The following passages are based on Chubei II's memoirs of his mother.

Yae was a hardy and very healthy woman. She was educated in a private elementary school (*terakoya*) where she learned reading, writing and arithmetic. She further learned to write Arabic numerals from her husband Chubei after marriage. She was skilled in arithmetic, and those who knew her were always impressed by her good memory. She possessed a moral and incorruptible character backed by a strong will, and was a lifelong,

Photograph of Yae

devout follower of Jodo Shinshu Buddhism.

In work, Yae was highly dexterous and extremely industrious. She married Chubei during his itinerant trading days before he opened his store in Osaka, and the two built their capital from scratch together as a couple. After Chubei opened his Osaka store, Yae stayed behind to care for their primary residence in Toyosato in the district of Inukami in Ohmi, and oversaw all the branch stores. She managed the procurement of the rice and barley used at the Osaka store, together with the polishing of the rice, the making of the miso, the pickling of *daikon* radishes and plums, and the selection of tea and tobacco. She also ensured all these various goods were shipped to Osaka.

In the winter, she managed the arrangement of great numbers of undershirts, kimonos, *obi* belts and aprons for the many apprentices, and in the summer she supervised the re-stuffing and washing of the futons. Yae was a true partner in Chubei's work.

Chubei's faith and satisfaction in his wife never changed throughout their marriage. The following three principles written by Chubei illustrate how deeply he cared for his wife. He would share these with people from time to time as secrets for success in life.

One, love your abode
Two, love your work
Three, love your wife

This means that to live a fulfilling and satisfying life, one should live somewhere they love, devote themselves to work that they love, and live together with a spouse with whom they share mutual understanding and affection. Married to Chubei, a man who would at times unabashedly express his affection publicly, Yae happily served her husband at home, a place where he could be very commanding and animated. A wife's role was to know her husband's strengths and weaknesses better than anyone else. While Yae was a woman who was unperturbed by matters around her, and did not easily succumb to difficulty, she also followed her husband devotedly.

Chubei and Yae arrived at a natural division of roles in the education of their children. Chubei was as harsh as the blazing sun to his son Seiichi, who would succeed him, but extremely doting on his daughters, to the point where he may have never even scolded them once in his life. Yae was the exact opposite, very tolerant towards her son, but firmly strict with her daughters.

Yae lived a long, full life, passing away in 1952 at the age of 104. Her memory remained sharp until her later years, and even when she received a visit from the governor of Shiga Prefecture after turning 100, she still personally directed the arrangement of tea and dishes to welcome him personally.

8. The Merchant Way and Faith

Ohmi merchants were people with a strong religious faith. The inside cover of the central ledger of the Takada Zenemon merchant house was inscribed with the quote, "Shinto, Confucianism, and Buddhism—worship all humbly." The next page detailed the house's donations to the three religions, with its regular accounting following thereafter. In addition to Shinto, Confucianism, and Buddhism, Ohmi merchants also venerated their ancestors. They devoted themselves to carrying out Buddhist memorial services and visiting the graves of their ancestors to rejoice in their deeds, pray for their protection, and give thanks for their blessings. Through their family precepts, however, the Ohmi merchants also taught their descendants that excessive worship and donating family treasures to temples and shrines was a mistake, and that devoting themselves first and foremost to carrying on their long-established family businesses and securing their livelihood fulfilled the wishes of the *kami* and buddhas.

Ito Chubei I was among the Ohmi merchants who believed that following the righteous "Way of the Merchant" was the same as following the Way of the Bodhisattva, and this conviction served as a motivation for his devotion to his family business. He was a faithful follower of Jodo Shinshu Buddhism, and was fond of visiting eminent Buddhist priests at the various destinations of his itinerant trading. He believed trading to be the way of the bodhisattva, referring to the bodhisattva to attain one's own enlightenment while bringing others to the same attainment. He founded his trading prin-

ciples on Buddhism. Viewing Buddhism as a means by which he could
motivate his employees, Chubei provided them with the book *Shoshinge-
wasan*, which explained the teachings
of Shinran, the founder of Jodo Shinshu Buddhism, together with a set of
prayer beads. Morning and evening,
all employees would join together in

Shoshinge-wasan

offering prayers at the Buddhist altar in the store. In his testament to his son,
Chubei wrote, "Even if you were to lose all your businesses and assets, you
must not lose your faith in the power of the Buddha."

The strength of the Ohmi merchants' faith was of course influenced by
their religious home environment, but it also represented their need for spiritual support in maintaining their family businesses, and achieving lofty goals
nearly unattainable by the power of a single individual. Their faith also served
as a strong support in the challenging management of their businesses. The
faith of the Ohmi merchants did more than suppress vice, prevent the needless
loss of assets and support the continuation of their businesses. As they entered
unknown lands and crossed seas, snowy plains, dark roads, and mountain
passes alone to make their fortunes, the Ohmi merchants' faith also served
as a means of seeking much-needed protection from disaster and injury that
bolstered their courage. This is the reason Ohmi merchants carried a small
lacquered box containing Buddhist statue with them wherever they went.

While the motivation differs slightly, the relation between the Ohmi
merchants' faith and their family businesses, and their belief that devoting
themselves to their work fulfilled the wishes of a higher power, bears some
resemblance to Protestant Puritanism which is said to form the spiritual base
of modern capitalism.

As we have seen, Chubei, who cherished harmonious marital relations
and held a strong faith, based his innovative management principles first and
foremost on providing satisfaction and happiness to his employees. No matter what example we look at, such as his hiring of young employees, pro-

viding *sukiyaki* feasts free from strict etiquette, applying equal travel expense rules to all employees, his solemn but heartfelt censuring of employees, deciding commercial policy through management meetings, dividing his profits three ways, or promoting spirituality through Buddhist teachings, all of Chubei's practices were rooted in his conviction that employee satisfaction leads to business prosperity. In terms of character, Ito Chubei can be considered an excellent manager who motivated his employees to work based on satisfaction, and a supreme educator possessed with great dignity.

A small lacquered box containing a Buddhist statue

CHAPTER

4

Insights from Management Philosophy

1 *Sanno-yoshi* and the Awareness of Being an Outsider

As stated previously, the linen trader Nakamura Jihei Sogan from Ishibaji in the district of Kanzaki was the first Ohmi trader to put the spirit of *sanpo-yoshi* into writing. Sogan, who lost both his wife and son, included the teachings of *sanpo-yoshi* in a will he left to his 15-year-old adoptive heir, Sojiro, in 1754. In the passage that serves as the basis for *sanpo-yoshi*, Sogan seeks to teach Sojiro that when trading in other provinces, it is vital that he hold the conviction that his products serve the people, and that he should always consider the perspective of others, without being swayed by the pursuit of profits. The will Sogan wrote to his young heir is imbued with his passion to convey the essence of trading he had learned through his own experience.

Signature of Nakamura Jihei Sogan

The passage of Sogan's will that refers to *sanpo-yoshi* became widely known in 1890 when Inoue Masatomo, the first author to publish a book related to Ohmi merchants in his work *Ohmi Shonin*, summarized Sogan's passage as follows: "When trading in other provinces, do not think only of yourself, but think of all the people in that place, do not covet personal profit, and never forget the *kami* and buddhas." It is believed that the expression *sanpo-yoshi* was derived from Inoue's summary, and we can thus see that the essence of the Ohmi merchant's management philosophy had already survived the test of time, as it was still embraced over one hundred years after it had first been put into writing.

Everyone who worked in the stores of the Ohmi merchants, from senior managers to the lowest ranked apprentices, was an outsider in the province where their store was located. It goes without saying that, as outsiders, these workers from Ohmi had to understand that their position differed from that of the local merchants. Ohmi merchants had a powerful awareness of being an outsider (*yosomono-ishiki*) to the extent that Ohmi merchants represent-

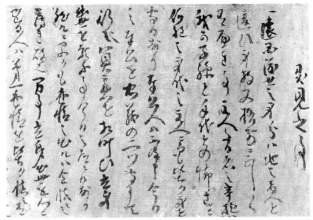

"The Awareness of
Being an Outsider" by
Yao Kihei IV

ing the preeminent trading house of Yao Kihei demanded their employees strictly manage their conduct with the full awareness that they were foreign merchants, even in stores that had been in business in the region for over a hundred years. This awareness led to management practices among Ohmi merchants that reflected their ongoing awareness of coexisting with the local people and caring for the local community. They were fully aware that without *sanpo-yoshi*, their business had no chance of success.

2. Appropriate Profits

Companies and corporations are organizations formed for the purpose of generating a profit. Business profits easily elicit greed, and can lead to the pursuit of personal profit. A store or corporation will soon lose its reason for being if it cannot justify the profits generated. How was the concept of profit viewed by the Ohmi merchants, whose vast knowledge led to the creation of the *sanpo-yoshi* philosophy that considered the perspective of not only the buyer and seller, but also a third party, namely the community, in transactions?

In the warrior, farmer, craftsman and merchant social hierarchy of feudal Japan, merchants were considered the lowest social rank due to their pursuit of profit, which was believed to arise from personal greed.

Samurai and Confucianist statesmen of the day viewed merchants as largely a useless but necessary evil. For example, the essayist writing under the pseudonym Buyo Inshi wrote in *Seji-kenbunroku* (An Account of What I Have Seen and Heard), stated, "merchants are well-nigh bandits, and have little chance of success if they do not possess the character of thieves and beggars." Buyo disparaged the Ohmi and Ise merchants, the leading merchants of the Edo period, as "Ohmi thieves and Ise beggars."

The reality of the Edo period was, however, that a social economy already existed that was beyond the easy control of the government, and merchants were an essential part of its makeup. One fundamental reason was that the ruling class, such as the shogun, and daimyo received their annual tax (*nengu*) in the form of rice, but needed to sell the majority of it to acquire currency to pay for their yearly expenses.

All the same, Sekimon Shingaku (literally, Sekimon's Heart Teachings), a popular teaching founded by Ishida Baigan (1685–1744) which exerted a great influence on commoners, unequivocally validated the pursuit of profit by merchants. It taught that the merchants and craftsmen who lived in the towns were the retainers of everyday life, just as the samurai were retainers of their lords, and were equal to them in both character and vocation. Further, it said that merchants' profits were comparable with samurai stipends, and asserted that if merchants were denied profits, so should samurai be denied stipends. Expecting merchants to work without profit would be like expecting samurai to serve

Ishida Baigan   The birthplace of Ishida Baigan

their lord without their stipend, which would mean a loss of livelihood. The Sekimon Shingaku teachings advocated that the profits gained by merchants were a legitimate stipend earned through sincere contribution to society.

Ohmi merchants were true practitioners of Sekimon Shingaku. *Chushi [Nakai] seiyo* (Essential Rules of Nakai), family precepts attributed to the Hino merchant Nakai Genzaemon II, offered the following thoughts on appropriate profits: "To live is to work, work is the source of profit, and that which you gain from good work is true profit." This passage assumes readers will lead a diligent, hard-working life, and states that if they work diligently and sincerely, they will not struggle in life due to lack of income, and will obtain true profits that would be questioned by no one. The same income, if it is obtained through market manipulation or speculation, and does not consider the hardship of others, is not considered true profit, and will not sustain the family business. The precepts warn that if readers leave their greed untamed, and seek profits outside the realm of reason, they will one day meet great hardship.

To the extent profits stimulated human greed, Ohmi merchants committed themselves to earning legitimate profits, and by so doing did all they could to maintain the family businesses built up over generations.

3. Avoid Waste and Give Your All

The Ohmi merchants who traded throughout all the provinces of Japan carrying their trusty *tenbinbo* poles placed the highest importance on devoting themselves to frugality by avoiding unnecessary expenses, and increasing their income through hard work. This was expressed in their daily creed, "avoid waste and give your all" (*shimatsu shite kibaru*).

Originally, *shimatsu* means to tie the beginning and end of a matter together into a conclusion. Instead of this typical usage, however, Ohmi merchants used the term *shimatsu* to emphasize using things without waste and being frugal. They handled everything, down to the simplest items of daily life such as a single sheet of paper, with the greatest of care, and also abhorred wasting time.

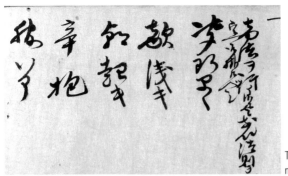

The daily creed of the Ohmi merchants

The historical surveys of the main residences of Ohmi merchants have revealed an astounding number of examples where even a trifling scrap of paper was carefully saved. In one case, even a sheet of paper, entirely blackened by its use for practicing calligraphy, was kept for safekeeping. The Ohmi merchants felt the greatest disgust at useless expenditure. All the same, they did not overly try to avoid expenditure. They fully understood that when it came to goods they used daily, such as clothing or building materials, choosing well-made, durable goods, even if they were expensive, would allow those items to be used well into the future and lead to true profit.

A lifestyle that reduced consumption and used items to their greatest utility was both the first and last goal, the *shimatsu* of Ohmi merchants. Considering the problems related to resources and the environment today, the attitude towards consumption evinced by the Ohmi merchants is still highly relevant.

The word *kibaru* is used as part of a daily greeting in modern-day Shiga Prefecture. *Okibariyasu* is the traditional greeting used when meeting others on the roadside, congratulating the other person for being able to work vigorously and in good health. It goes without saying that Ohmi merchants, born in a region where work was part of daily conversation, were exceptionally diligent. Their diligence is symbolized by their practice of setting out with their shoulder poles while the stars could still be seen in the dawn sky, and only returning home by starlight after a full day of trading. This is one reason the word *hoshi* ("star") can be seen in the names of many of the stores opened by Ohmi merchants, such as Yamaboshi, Kaneboshi, Maruboshi or Hoshikyu.

A record has even been found concerning the distance one Ohmi merchant walked in a single year of itinerant selling, a clear illustration of their great diligence. Okui Mango, a cotton and linen kimono trader from Kawanami in the district of Kanzaki, recollected in 1893 that in one year he twice made the 800 kilometer journey from Ohmi to northern Japan. During that same period, he also travelled along the Sanindo Road to the Izumo and

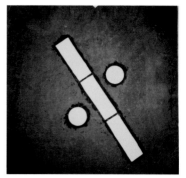

Stencil of the Hoshikyu trademark

Hoki regions in modern-day Shimane and Tottori Prefectures to purchase cotton goods. He thus walked a total of 1,000 *ri*, or 4,000 kilometers, in a single year. Even if one assumes that Okui spent every day of the year traveling, this would mean that he walked over ten kilometers a day. Furthermore, when one considers that he must have travelled this entire distance carrying a shoulder pole with eleven to fifteen kilograms of goods, he must certainly have been a good walker.

The Ohmi merchants truly demonstrated through their activities that they were diligent, hard-working individuals, imbued with a frugality that paid great respect to avoiding waste.

4. The Determination to Start a Business

The life histories of Ohmi merchants are an invaluable source of information when trying to understand their character. A similar idea applies to companies. The essence of an organization is often already exhibited at the time of its founding. What motivated the Ohmi merchants to enter the commercial world?

The Shono Genzo family from Hino in Gamo district is a venerable family with a long history. Kannogan, a traditional medicine still sold today, was manufactured for generations by this family. Genzo I (1659–1733), the third son of a farming family, began peddling at the age of eighteen. He used the

money he accumulated through peddling to undertake training in medicine in
Kyoto in 1693, and then went on to create
the renowned Kannogan medicine.

When he first started peddling, Genzo
combined his accounts with that of his
family, but after eight years of trading,
his father advised him to start trading
independently, and Genzo thus set off to
the Shinano and Echigo regions of central

Shono Genzo I

Japan, over 400 kilometers from his birthplace in Hino, to establish himself as
an independent peddler of clothing.

He took this opportunity to begin recording his sales in his own central
account book, starting in 1684. This account book was Genzo's most important possession. On its inside cover, he wrote a set of reminders (*oboe*) that
was a virtual resolution for setting out as an independent peddler. He wrote:

"I received all my seed capital as loans from relatives, and had absolutely no personal capital. I must pay careful attention to repaying these
loans without taking advantage of our connections. If I am unable to
repay my loans due to unforeseen expenses, I am determined to ensure
the full payment of my loans, even if I have to cease my independent
peddling and become an employee of another house. Even if I come to
accumulate my own capital, I will not employ any apprentices (*tedai*)
until I have saved 100 *ryo*. Even if I am one day fortunate enough to
be able to build my own house, I will not allow the building expenses
to exceed one-tenth of my personal capital. I will never fail to clearly
record my profit and loss in December, by recording my net assets at the
start and end of the given year."

Based on this resolution, Genzo gathered a total of 400 *ryo* or approximately
40 million yen from his relatives with the assistance of his two older brothers
and mother, and was thus blessed with sufficient capital when he first estab-

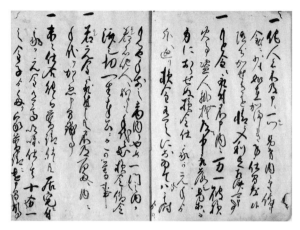

Shono Genzo's proclamation to found his business

lished his trading. This capital enabled him to immediately begin moving large quantities of goods in the manner of a wholesaler, granting him equal opportunities for wealth. Genzo would go on to save 600 *ryo* over the course of ten years, thus accumulating sufficient capital to enter into medical training.

By demonstrating his own voluntary abstinence as part of his powerful desire to achieve independence, Genzo was able to garner support from those around him, which allowed him to introduce advantageous trading practices from the very outset of his business.

5. The Spirit of the Peddler

Aspiring Ohmi merchants had two paths to enter the world of business. One was to set out peddling, and the other was to become the employee of an established trading house. If an individual chose to start with peddling, they had no one to teach them, and therefore had to grow bit by bit through a process of daily trial and error. What kind of spirit did these Ohmi merchants who set out independently with shoulder poles have?

One merchant who helps illustrate this spirit is Kobayashi Ginemon from the Chojiya store in Kotakari in Echi district. Ginemon was known by his nickname Chogin, and as a silk, cotton and linen kimono wholesaler, he became one of the most prominent and wealthy merchants of the nineteenth century.

Kobayashi Ginemon I (1777–1854) started peddling when he was twenty-two years old. Trading in textiles and sundry goods, he peddled among nearby villages, and over his long life expanded his reach towards the Tokaido Road. A few months before Ginemon passed away, he was visited at his main residence in Kotakari by Yao Kihei IV, who had a branch

Illustration of Kobayashi Ginemon I

store in the Chichibu region of Musashi Province, to discuss a regional currency exchange initiative. Kihei, who was a prolific writer, recorded the words of Ginemon in a memorandum entitled *Kenbun zuihitsu* (Essays on What I Have Seen and Heard).

"It is vain and futile to toil carrying a shoulder pole while dreaming of becoming a prominent merchant from the very beginning. Everyone has some ambition, but it is not enough to work only with ambition. A minor merchant who still lacks the capital to have his own store, and instead peddles carrying a shoulder pole, relies on the favor and support of others to sustain his daily life. Therefore, if one is not sincere in thinking of the position of others, they will not lend you their support. On the other hand, if you devote yourself first of all to never cheating others, and never hesitate to work with all your might, the hearts of others will be naturally moved by your sincerity and diligence. If you can make that impression upon others, your business will go well, and your assets will grow before you know it. Luck also plays a certain role in life, so it is important to be blessed with good fortune as well."

Kenbun zuihitsu

These words by Ginemon demonstrate the spirit of the Ohmi merchants by clarifying the differences in how Ohmi merchants and poor peddlers approach the same business of trading carrying a shoulder pole. Ginemon clearly states

that if a person wishes to prosper as an Ohmi merchant, it is far more important to always consider his surroundings and others in business, and strive to
serve society, than simply toiling with a raw ambition to become a major merchant, even when starting out as a minor peddler.

All aspiring merchants climbed a path of grit and diligence, fully aware
that they were members of society, as they sought to reach the lofty heights of
being an Ohmi merchant.

6. Faith and Devotion

Ohmi merchants were not only passionate about their business, but they
were also deeply religious. They were no doubt influenced by the religious
character of Ohmi Province itself, which is home to many influential temples and shrines known throughout Japan, such as the temples of Enryakuji
and Miidera, and Hiyoshi Taisha Shrine. Temples and shrines can also
be found in almost every village, and many festivals and Buddhist rites
reflecting the nature of Ohmi have been passed down to the present. The
family precepts recorded by the Tonomura Yozaemon house state: "One
should respect shrines and temples, always adhere to the Buddhist teachings, faithfully act with loyalty and filial piety, maintain rigorous bodily
strength, and never forget to venerate the interior Buddha (the household
Buddhist altar) morning and evening." Even this brief passage teaches faith
in the three teachings of Shinto, Confucianism and Buddhism, as well as
ancestor veneration.

A large number of people in the Koto region of Ohmi Province, which
is the birthplace of many Ohmi merchants, practice Buddhism, in particular
Jodo Shinshu, and there are an accordingly large number of Ohmi merchants
who were devout followers of this Buddhist sect. Jodo Shinshu taught that
anyone could be reborn in paradise through absolute faith in Amida Buddha,
the savior of all believers. The Pure Land ideal of Jodo Shinshu encourages
people to devote themselves to their family business as an expression of gratitude that they are enabled to be reborn in paradise. These teachings led to
the shunning of fraud, greed, and wanton luxury as abhorrent qualities. In

that sense, the religious and business ethics of
Ohmi merchants were very much aligned with
the precepts of Jodo Shinshu Buddhism.

Ono Zensuke I, born in Omizo-cho in
Takashima district, who went on to become the
head of the Ono-gumi association, engaged in
trade between northern Japan and the capital
region, basing himself in the Morioka region
and Kyoto. He wrote in his testament that if
one rigorously followed the teachings of Jodo

Shichiri Kojun

Shinshu passed down by the ancestors in private, and adhered to the virtues
of benevolence, righteousness, propriety, knowledge and sincerity taught by
Confucius in public, that person would be assured comfort both in this life
and in the hereafter.

Further, Nakamura Jihei Sogan recommended in the will he left to his
adoptive heir in 1754 that he pray to the *kami* and buddhas every morning
when washing his face. By thus making reverence and praying to avoid vice,
he can live a healthy life in both mind and body.

Ito Chubei I interpreted faith as a more active and personal endeavor.
When Chubei travelled to the western reaches of Japan in his itinerant trading, he always visited the eminent priest Shichiri Kojun of the Jodo Shinshu
temple Mangyoji in Hakata to receive his teachings. Chubei later recalled
that when he opened his store in Osaka in 1872, while he did not in the least
hesitate relinquishing to his brother the commercial area he had personally
developed in Kyushu, he was devastated that he could no longer receive the
Buddhist teachings of Shichiri Kojun.

Tsukamoto Sadaemon I also recommended religious faith and listening to
religious teachings, stating, "If you are born into this world as a human, it is
perilous to live without something to believe in. Whether young or old, people should entrust their soul to religion."

For Ohmi merchants seeking commercial success, their devout faith combined a standard encouraging humility and the avoidance of vice with prayers
for the continuation of the family businesses.

7. Social Contribution by Corporations

The French word *mécénat*, which originally meant supporting arts and culture, has been adopted in Japan and used to refer to the corporate patronage of culture and activities to support local communities. The word is derived from Maecenas, a patron of the arts under the first Roman emperor Augustus. In the 1970s, Japanese corporations developed a greater awareness of *mécénat*, and it was particularly popular during the economic bubble of the latter half of the 1980s. After the collapse of the bubble, and the long recession that followed, many companies found themselves forced to abandon their *mécénat* activities. The cancelation of the Asian Mécénat Conference, scheduled to be held in Melbourne in 1998, demonstrated the weakness of corporate *mécénat*, which was highly dependent on the business health of the corporation.

Recently, however, there has been renewed interest among investment trust companies in investing in corporations that emphasize social contributions as well as legal compliance and environmental conservation, demonstrating a perspective that accounts for both social responsibility and profitability. We are now in an age where people do not only seek profitability from corporate management, but also consider whether the company is maintaining a good relationship with society in some form. This can be considered a sign of society's growing maturity.

In response to this trend, there are companies now steadily promoting initiatives in regional vitalization and cultural development. This is a form of community-based *mécénat* activity.

Many examples exist of this new form of *mécénat* activity. For example, one company has repurposed old houses in Japan's "snow country" region, part of the Shirakawa-go and Gokayama UNESCO World Heritage site, to serve as training facilities, while preserving them in their original form. It has thus revitalized important cultural properties that were in danger of being abandoned. The houses now serve as a base for employees to participate in group work such as weed cutting and shoveling snow from the roofs of the houses. In addition to contributing to society, these activities also foster team spirit. Another company contributes to the preservation of traditional crafting techniques by supporting the construction of festival floats. At yet another company, on a set date and time, all employees, including the president, put on gloves and carry plastic bags, and work up a sweat carrying out local cleanup activities as part of employee development.

Mécénat often evokes the image of enormous companies investing large amounts of money in spectacular activities, but more attention should be paid to the locally focused, diligent activities carried out by small and medium enterprises (SMEs). The Ohmi merchants, who established stores throughout Japan while maintaining their main residences in Ohmi, were also always concerned for the people both in their hometown and the regions in which they opened their stores, and made great efforts to build healthy relationships in these regions.

Yao Kihei IV from Hino warned his employees at the Chichibu branch store in Musashi Province, which had been open for over a hundred years, to never forget that they were outsiders in the province. His mindset resembled the very essence of *mécénat*. Some noteworthy examples of *mécénat* carried out by Ohmi merchants include renovating the Setanokarahashi Bridge, and constructing a wagon road of granite flagstones on Mt. Osaka, which formed the border between Kyoto and Ohmi Province, and had been a critical junction since ancient times, with a checkpoint at its base. Modern examples include Furukawa Tetsujiro, an executive director of Marubeni, building the Toyosato Elementary School.

Despite being faced with substantial financial burdens, modern companies that can trace their lineage to Ohmi merchants are still investing money in maintaining the former homes of Ohmi merchants such as the Ohmi Merchant

The Ohmi Merchants Local Museum

Jushin-an

Local Museum in Kotakari-cho and Jushin-an in Kawanami-cho in the city of Higashiohmi and the Nishikawa Cultural Foundation in Osugi-cho in the city of Ohmihachiman, and opening them to the public. These activities represent praiseworthy acts of *mécénat* that embody the spirit of their ancestors.

8. Customer Satisfaction

There is something I am reminded of every year on university graduation day, when I see the elaborate kimonos worn by the graduating female students. While these luxurious kimonos are of course the appropriate attire for such a celebratory day, to the parents of the students, they represent an additional expense on top of the tuition they have already paid for four years. I feel great empathy for both their happiness and the enormous economic burden this custom must present. My anxiety, may however, simply be misplaced. Instead of being purchased by the parents, who are facing the peak of their mortgage loan payments, these kimonos might be gifts gladly given by the grandparents, who have greater financial freedom to dote on their beloved granddaughters.

Among the healthy elderly people today, there are many who have financial freedom and are enjoying life. Looking at the increasing number of people taking overseas trips every year, I see growing numbers of elderly couples relaxing in business class seats, looking forward to broadening their horizons on journeys planned with specific goals in mind. The key consideration driving personal consumption has been shifting from simple price to quality. Companies that skillfully capture this trend have the opportunity to enhance customer satisfaction.

One example can be found in men's clothing. Customers are seeking to enjoy the texture and appearance of their clothing in an entirely different way from just look-

A university graduation ceremony

ing to have the necessary sets of work clothing. Customer satisfaction will undoubtedly be enhanced if couples can go out on their days off, and leisurely browse the products of different businesses in wide, open spaces without being hounded by shop clerks. Customers who shop in this way would, on the whole, not be unduly influenced by ever-changing trends, making it easy for shops to convert them into fixed customers.

Other examples of original ideas that solve the problems faced by customers include luxury travel plans targeting an audience that seeks genuine experiences, healthy and reasonably-priced dishes that can be enjoyed by many people, children's clothing and insurance. Developing unique products such as these from the customer's perspective and enhancing customer satisfaction by respecting their views represents a far-sighted and deeply insightful marketing strategy.

As mentioned previously, the management philosophy that emphasizes thoroughly understanding and respecting the position of the customer, can be found in the testament of Nakamura Jihei Sogan, which serves as the original source of *sanpo-yoshi*. Additionally, the following passage from the Nishikawa Jingoro merchant house family precepts always appeared on the back cover of the ledger (*kanjo-mokuroku-cho*) prepared annually by the Edo branch of the Nishikawa merchant house to record the key transactions of the store throughout the year for submission to the head of the house.

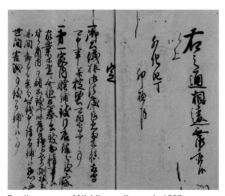

Family precept of Nishikawa Jingoro in 1807

Nishikawa Jingoro's birth place

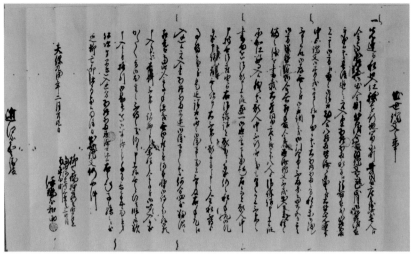

Shusse-shomon

"As all employees sleep and eat together in the same house, we will deepen our friendship with one another, and devote all our efforts to advancing the family business. When selling goods, we will offer high quality products that have been carefully examined for the lowest commission possible. Even when supplies are low between ship deliveries, we will not take more than the necessary commission. No matter what comes to pass, we will not undertake any actions that harm the world."

The stoic attitude that a seller should not take extra commission even when stock is low is the essence of a sales strategy that emphasizes customer satisfaction over personal profit.

9. Corporate Social Responsibility

"Corporate social responsibility" (CSR) has entered the Japanese lexicon in recent years. This is something that has been talked about for a long time, and one might expect that there is little room for this concept to develop further. In reality, however, while the word has remained the same, the concept has changed greatly over time.

Until recently, the social contribution that made up CSR was viewed as a passive cost, comprised of offering economic value, preventing scandals, and ensuring legal compliance. Today, however, CSR is viewed as a corporate strategy for proactively responding to changes in society.

This concept emerged in the midst of high unemployment, climate change, shocking events such as the 9/11 terror attacks in 2001, and cases of accounting fraud by major corporations such as Enron and WorldCom. The 9/11 terror attack on the World Trade Center in New York was an act of terrorism on a scale that had never been seen before, and could be considered an irrational reaction to global corporate activity. Cases of companies falling into bankruptcy can be viewed as the result of corporations blindly pursuing short-term profit while ignoring their relationship with society.

Looking at the changes in today's society from the perspective of market influence, we can see that together with the increased globalization of corporate activity, and the diversification of values, the influence of consumers is becoming larger than that of producers. In other words, going forward, consumers will not only demand that corporations provide economic value, but that they also increase their social value. Corporate management that ignores this will be doomed to fail. To that end, corporations now see CSR as an investment that helps them achieve sustainable growth instead of simply a cost, and as an activity that must be given a core position in their business management. Doing so will allow corporations to reduce the myriad risks they face, and also allow them to create new markets ahead of others.

The *sanpo-yoshi* management philosophy of the Ohmi merchants, which emphasized "Good for the seller, good for the buyer, and good for the world," strongly mirrors the tenets of CSR. Talented Ohmi merchants devoted themselves to proactively contributing to society. As we have seen, Nakai Shojiemon from Hino obtained permission from the *bakufu* to rebuild Setano-karahashi in 1815, which required an astonishing sum of money, three billion yen in today's terms. Tsukamoto Sadaemon II from Kawanami used his financial strength not only to preserve mountains and rivers, but also to provide an educational grant of 10,000 yen (approximately 200 million yen today) to the Shiga Prefecture Commercial School in 1900. Both of these individuals were extremely capable managers, who brought about large-scale growth in their businesses. This suggests there may be a synergistic link between social contribution and corporate management.

10. Disposing of Debts, *Orei-shomon* and *Shusse-shomon*

When travelling abroad, advertisements of Japanese companies can be found everywhere in the downtown and upscale districts of major cities. Most of the advertisements, however, are for manufacturing companies. The major banks of Japan, which hold some of the highest deposits in the world, are almost never seen. This is because Japanese banks are not yet ready to expand their core banking businesses abroad, nor to take part in the fierce competition at the global level. The primary hurdle to their entry is likely the problem of nonperforming loans.

At the end of March 2003, the issue of nonperforming loans at Japanese banks was thought to be on the verge of bringing about a new financial disaster. This dire view was only dispelled in May of the same year, when public funds were injected to prevent the dissolution of Resona Bank. Now, in 2004, concerns over the problem of nonperforming loans have largely dissipated, and the stock prices of major banks have risen to their highest levels in the year to date.

Just because fears of a financial crisis have abated, however, does not mean the issue of nonperforming loans that developed over the past ten years will be suddenly resolved. That is because the fundamental mechanism that leads to nonperforming loans, such as long-running unfavorable conditions driving a previously healthy borrower into nonperformance, or existing nonperforming loans further deteriorating and thus generating new nonperforming loans, remain unaddressed.

In order to achieve the final disposal of nonperforming loans, laws such as the Corporate Rehabilitation Act and the Civil Rehabilitation Act have been amended, financial aid for abandoned claims is available, rehabilitation funds have been recently established, and the Industrial Revitalization Corporation has begun efforts to revive corporations carrying excessive debt and speed up the disposal of nonperforming loans.

The issue lies in the fact that financial institutions that receive public funds agree to the requests of debt-loaded corporations to dispose of their loans. Furthermore, under the modern abandonment of debts, the corporation requesting the disposal has no obligation to repay the disposed debts even if its situation improves in the future. Taxpayers have simple but nonetheless serious concerns regarding this system. At the very least, the managers of these corporations should be strictly called into question over their management responsibilities.

Ohmi merchants, who were defined by their diverse business ventures, were also involved in the finance industry, operating as pawnbrokers and money changers (*ryogaesho*). This also entailed the writing of loans, and many bonds of debt still exist today. Among those documents, *orei-shomon* and *shusse-shomon* in particular are unique. The *orei-shomon* is a statement of gratitude offered to the lender when they accept the request of a borrower to dispose of their debt because they can no longer make repayments, and the *shusse-shomon* is a document by which the debtor promises to one day pay back the debt when they achieve success in the world.

Matsui Yuken of Inde in Kanzaki district was a merchant of legendary talent and virtue, who increased his assets from 7,600 *ryo* at the time he inherited them to 83,000 *ryo* at the time of his death at 86 in 1855. The amount of debt Matsui waived throughout his life reached seven percent of his assets, or 5,800 *ryo* (approximately 280 million yen). Matsui, however, did not simply dispose of this debt. Rather, he converted these loans to those that could be repaid when the borrower achieved success in the world, thus providing encouragement to his borrowers and discretely demonstrating his virtue.

11. "Construction During Famine" and "Helping Construction"

While modern Japan may experience poor rice harvests, it is unlikely to ever lead to a famine. 1993 was a year of a poor harvest and the government's stock of rice was entirely depleted. During this time, while the price of rice skyrocketed regardless of quality, people remember that crisis was averted by importing rice from Thailand.

Looking back over the various decades in the history of modern Japan, the Showa depression in the 1930s and the aftermath of World War II were times of severe food shortage akin to a famine. The Edo period, a time when information and logistics were far less developed than today, saw the outbreak of many severe famines. Five famines stand out for their severity: the Kanei famine of 1642, the Kyoho famine of 1732, the Horeki famine of 1755, the Tenmei famine from 1783 to 1787, and the Tempo famine from 1833 to 1837.

As a result of these famines, people in villages and towns rioted, seeking reduction of taxes and the price of rice. The Edo shogunate and individual *han* governments responded by establishing relief facilities (*osukuigoya*) to distribute rice to the population. At the same time, the stockpiling of rice and grain was prohibited, and violators were sought out and exposed. The export of rice to other provinces was also forbidden.

Ohmi merchants, who had expanded their business throughout Japan, distributed rice and money from their branch stores and main residences when such famines occurred, out of a desire to help the poor. Nakai Genzaemon, for example, distributed 350 *hyo* (approximately 2,000 kg) of rice at his Sendai branch store during the Tempo famine, and circulated flyers stating it would pay for the treatment of infectious diseases.

During the Tempo famine, Fujino Shirobei VII, for example, built his main residence in his hometown of Hie in Echi district to help the poor by creating work. The Fujino house achieved great success at the advent of the nineteenth century through its fishing business in Hokkaido. Shirobei improved the kombu seaweed harvesting and salmon fishing techniques in Nemuro in Hokkaido, and rapidly expanded the family business to open stores in Matsumae and Hakodate. During the Tempo famine, he donated and sold rice at exceedingly low prices at his store in Matsumae. At the same time he renovated his main residence in Ohmi, and also sponsored the repair of a Buddhist temple. When the daimyo of Hikone domain came to

Fujino Shirobei VII

Komori Kyuzaemon's Saitama brewery and warehouse

know of Shirobei's construction plans, he at first sent magistrates to denounce Shirobei for his callous extravagance during a time of hardship. Shirobei, however, explained his true intention, which was to provide relief and care not just by offering money but by providing work as well, and that in addition to paying his workers, he also provided rice porridge to their families When the lord of Hikone domain came to know of this, he was greatly moved and praised Shirobei. This beautiful, virtuous deed came to be known among the people as "Fujino's Construction during the Famine," and has been passed down and praised through generations.

Another virtuous deed was performed by Komori Kyuzaemon from Hino in 1886, when the deflationary policies of the Finance Minister Matsukata Masayoshi led to a severe depression. Kyuzaemon built a massive brewery warehouse of 200 *tsubo* (660 square meters) specifically in response to the crisis in Kisai-cho in modern-day Saitama Prefecture, where he had a branch store. This construction, which served to aid the poor, has long been praised as the "Helping Construction," a truly praiseworthy example of social contribution.

The "Famine Construction" and "Helping Construction" can be said to have taken the place of public works normally conducted by national and local authorities responsible for providing relief to the people during a poor harvest or financial depression. These works not only provided a non-repayable injection of funds, but also provided compensation to the laborers, demonstrating the great care Shirobei and Kyuzaemon paid to the position of others. This made their relief efforts stand out all the more.

Insights from Management Methods

1. Forced Dismissal of a Merchant House Head

The Ohmi merchants founded their family businesses on a philosophy of diligence and abstinence from greed, and a commitment to sincere contribution to society by facilitating the flow of goods throughout Japan. Accordingly, if the current head of a merchant house was considered an improper individual who posed a danger to their business, which had been built up through the accumulation of legitimate profits, the guardians and heads of related merchant houses would convene to forcibly dismiss the head of the troubled merchant house through a process known as *oshikome-inkyo*.

Forced dismissal or compulsory retirement was an uncommon and drastic course of action. In today's terms, it would be the equivalent of the forced dismissal of the president of a company. This process of forced dismissal was required as an emergency measure, however, to ensure the continuity of the business.

The need to occasionally resort to a forced dismissal in response to a scandal can be clearly seen in examples provided by two of Japan's long-standing department store chains. When the Mitsukoshi Department Store (now Isetan Mitsukoshi Holdings Ltd.) board of directors made the snap decision to force out its dogmatic president, it provided the chance for a much-needed business revitalization. In comparison, when the Sogo Department Store (now Seibu & Sogo Co., Ltd.) board of directors failed to stop its dictatorial president, the results were tragic: the business collapsed and two vice-presidents committed suicide.

Oshikome-inkyo was a legitimate process clearly set down in the articles of the Ohmi merchant house family precepts. The following is a list of major merchant houses that stipulated forced dismissal within their family precepts:

Mitsukoshi Department Store

The Ono Zensuke House: Memoranda of 1717 and 1728
The Nishikawa Jingoro House: The Family
Precepts of 1799
The Nakai Genzaemon House: The House
Code of 1823
The Kobayashi Ginemon House:
The Shimeshiai-no-jomoku articles of 1850
The Tonomura Yozaemon House: The Sahoki
articles of 1856

Shimeshiai-no-jomoku articles

The *oshikome-inkyo* articles were not superficial stipulations, they were practical regulations put into practice when the situation demanded it. The eighth generation head of the Nishikawa Jingoro merchant house could not accustom himself to business, wasting large amounts of money and engaging in a form of misconduct known as "running away." He was accordingly forced out as the head of the family in 1813, eleven years after he assumed the post of head, as an admonishment from Nishikawa Jingoro VIII's father, who was the guardian (*kokenyaku*) of the affairs of the merchant house, relatives, and Nishikawa branch houses.

Another example of forced dismissal occurred in the Nakai Genzaemon merchant house. When improper dealings of the fourth generation adopted heir with the administration of Sendai domain led to the closing of the house's Sendai branch store, its crown jewel, he was forced out of his leadership role in 1861 by his employees' demand he be dismissed. In another case, although it did not result in a forced dismissal per se, when the business of the Yamanaka Hyoemon merchant house from Hino languished under the management of its young fourth generation head, Yamanaka Hyoemon, who was lacking in both training and experience, his employees banded together in 1829, headed by their senior managers, demanding he reform his ways and threatening that they would all resign if he did not do so. In response, Hyoemon pledged to reform.

These examples of forced dismissal show that the board of directors of the Ohmi merchant houses, consisting of guardians, relatives and branch houses, was functioning properly.

2. Talent and Innovation

Talent is the quality of being quick-witted and highly intelligent, and innovativeness is the quality of giving everything one has and trying various approaches to achieve a good result. Talent and innovation allow merchants to keenly sense commercial opportunities, skillfully formulate a business strategy, and bring innovative ideas together to achieve a profit.

Ihara Saikaku (1642–1693) was the author of Japan's first novels about the economy, including *Nippon Eitaigura* (The Eternal Storehouse of Japan) *Seken Munezanyo* (This Scheming World) and *Saikaku Oridome* (Saikaku's Final Weaving). Even his pen-name, Saikaku, which was a homonym for *saikaku*, meaning "talent," was a demonstration of his fascination with talent. He proposed that those who failed to achieve success despite working themselves to the bone were doomed by their lack of talent and innovation, and accordingly he loved to write tales of merchants who used their talent and innovation to rise to prominence.

When a young apprentice entered an Ohmi merchant house, one standard of his evaluation was whether he was useful or useless. This illustrates the importance Ohmi merchants placed on an individual being quick-witted and intelligent, as they considered it impossible to achieve wealth and prominence without talent and innovation. We will now present several episodes that demonstrate the talent and innovation of the Ohmi merchants.

The creative innovation of the Ohmi merchants can be seen in their determination to expand from Ohmi Province in central Japan all the way to Hokkaido in the north and Kyushu in the south to open up new markets from the early Edo period, a time during which the movement of goods and people was difficult and lodging was not readily available. Achieving such a difficult feat is proof of both their forward thinking and their tireless innovation. At the time, the consignment sales and regional product rotation trading method, which combined the trading of raw materials with their related finished products, created by the Ohmi merchants, also represented an entirely new axis of commercial development.

Some of the practical innovations Ohmi merchants made to sell their products include the *moegino kaya* mosquito nets sold by the Nishikawa Jingoro

The "Moegino Kaya" ukiyo-e print by Kitagawa Utamaro

merchant house. These nets, which featured *moegiji* fabric with a bright red outline, became such a definitive bedroom adornment that they were even featured in the ukiyo-e prints of the day. The Nishikawa merchant house established the foundation of its business by selling the nets through *uriko* sales clerks. The traditional herbal

Illustration of mosquito net merchants

medicine Kannogan, which is still sold today, was developed by the Shono Genzo merchant house. In addition to its medicinal effectiveness, it was given a sense of luxury by the application of an appealing half-moon shape and silver foil coating, which allowed Kannogan to be sold at a price ten times greater than that of regular medicines.

Matsui Yuken, the third generation head of the Matsui Kyuzaemon merchant house was one of the most prominent and prosperous Ohmi merchants of the late Edo period. At the time, *dachin uma*,

Kannogan medicine

Dachin uma

packhorses that would carry people and goods for a fee, carried loads of 40 *kanme* (150 kilograms) per horse. Many merchants, however, bundled their goods into shipments of 42–43 *kanme*, exceeding the limit for one horse.

Yuken went against this convention, fixing the loads of his shipments at 38 *kanme*. Moreover, he also offered the packhorse drivers a tip for each *ri* (approximately four kilometers) they traveled. This encouraged the drivers to compete to carry Yuken's goods, allowing his shipments to arrive at their destinations earlier than those of other merchants, thus enabling Yuken to swiftly sell his products. This innovation in shipment increased the turnover of products, and Yuken was able to rotate his goods three to four times a year, in comparison to the two rotations achieved by other merchants annually. Through the above examples we can see that talent and tireless innovation were essential elements of the Ohmi merchant's creativity.

3. Leveraging Information

The journeys made by Ohmi merchants were not only part of sales activities, but also important opportunities to gather information and develop commercial strategy. The trips taken by the heads of major merchant houses to visit several dozen of their most important clients were made not only to deepen these personal relationships, but also to gauge the level of trust with these key partners.

Nakai Genzaemon III left behind a detailed diary of a 38-day trip he made together with three companions in 1829 to visit his key clients in the Sendai region. From his diary, we know that Genzaemon lodged at the homes of his closest clients, and was

The travel diary of Nakai Genzaemon III

treated to a feast every day. His personal relationships were thus deepened even further. One particularly important feature of the diary is its detailed description of the number of houses in the towns and villages he passed through and of village and town boundaries. He also recorded minor details such as the number of tofu shops and public baths, the price of goods, and the currency exchange rates for gold and silver. He also went on to note the trees and shrubs native to each region, and notable features such as mines. It is clear that Genzaemon's journey served as both a thorough commercial survey and an opportunity to foster closer relationships.

Making sound decisions based on information gathered was also an important skill for Ohmi merchants. One illustrative tale can be found in the first itinerant trading trip to Edo made by Tonomura Yozaemon I in 1726. When Yozaemon set out to trade, he chose to change his course to the direction of Edo when he obtained information regarding the strong economy of the area around the Sekigahara post station on the Nakasendo Road. He employed a guide and traded his way to Edo, but when he arrived, he found that it was not possible to bypass the established wholesalers and sell directly to retail merchants. Faced with this unexpected turn, Yozaemon quickly pulled up his stakes and left Edo. This became a well-known story of commercial failure based on uncertain information, and represented a loss of 17 *ryo* for Yozaemon at the time.

In 1812, Tsukamoto Sadaemon I from Kawanami in Kanzaki district opened his first branch store in Kofu in Kai Province (Yamanashi Prefecture). This was motivated by Kofu being the town where Sadaemon sold the most *komachi-beni*, a high quality lip color, when he first started itinerant trading at the age of nineteen. Sadaemon discerned that if a premium product such as *komachi-beni* sold well, this was a sign of strong buying power in the region. Sadaemon's sales went on to grow steadily, and he added fiber goods to his line-up. Sadaemon further expanded with the opening of a Kyoto branch store and even entered the marine transport business.

Tsukamoto Sadaemon I

Amidst experiences of both success and failure, the Ohmi merchants devoted themselves to continuously innovating to acquire sound information. Travelling merchant unions, composed of members with differing destinations and hometowns, were able to systematically gather information, and partly served as an organization to utilize this valuable information.

One union that performed this function was the Hino-daitoban-nakama union composed of members from Hino and surrounding areas. This organization was founded on two pillars: its special permission from the shogunate in Edo to carry out procedures to collect accounts receivable in other provinces, and also a system that allowed merchants to use special lodging along the Tokaido and Nakasendo Roads, which provided both comfort and convenience when setting out on long trips. The organization also had a system to quickly process the information obtained by its various members. These examples show that the Ohmi merchants based their commercial strategy on the highly relational principle of gathering information and processing it in an intelligent, business savvy manner.

4. Investing in Startup Ventures

A major challenge when it comes to restoring and sustaining economic and social vigor, is being able to launch new startup ventures to meet demands that cannot be fulfilled by existing companies, and forming a system to value such ventures effectively. If one examines the major sources of venture capital funding by their investment goals, they can be divided into public organizations such as the central government and regional authorities, financial institutions and individual investors, and organizations that focus on socially responsible investing (SRI).

Public organizations primarily foster startup ventures as one aspect of their long-term economic policy.

Banks, financial institutions, and incubator funds founded by wealthy individuals invest in startup ventures that have already launched their business and plan to make a public stock offering in the future, or have a high possibility of eventually going public. In the event the startup venture targeted for investment does go public according to plan, the investors stand to reap profits amounting to multiple times their initial investment, regardless of share sales. Socially responsible investment is primarily carried out by non-profit and similar organizations, and focuses on not just the financials of a company, but whether its profits are increasing while adhering to social rules.

Evaluating startup ventures is a major challenge in venture investment. When making such an investment, there is always the risk that the venture will fail to succeed, making the investment worthless, and because the capital is provided as an investment instead of a loan, repayment cannot be sought.

Various venture evaluation systems have been formed to meet the critical challenge of evaluating startup ventures. These are organized by local authorities and financial institutions, made up of a committee of experts with rich business experience, who evaluate the future prospects of startup ventures, and certify companies that meet their standards. Startup ventures that are certified as being suitable for investment leverage this approval to obtain an advantageous position both in financing and market reception. Non-profit organizations have also been established to foster the growth of individual investors (angels) for startup ventures.

Startup ventures that receive these investments must look beyond just their technical prowess, and develop the appropriate human resources to effectively leverage the funds they gather without waste, and present a clear and transparent business plan. This will help make venture investing and funding a more familiar practice, and broaden its base of support.

It goes without saying that the Ohmi merchants, who founded a number of the oldest companies still in operation today, once had their own startup period. A point of commonality can be found between the various Ohmi merchant houses at the time of their founding. First, the founder had a powerful desire to achieve independence as a travelling merchant. These ambitious founders could seek loans from wealthy merchants in the area who saw promise in them, and also receive funding from *tanomoshi-ko* and *mujin-ko* associations, which were private organizations formed to provide reciprocal funding. All of the loans the Ohmi merchants received were interest-free or at most low-interest, which speaks to the close presence of supporters who could provide advantageous funding. The funds gathered in this way were then used in innovative commercial enterprises, such as consignment sales or the sale of goods through *uriko* sales clerks, or by joining a *noriai-akinai* joint venture.

5. Profitability and Corporate Value

The colorful hydrangeas that add delightful points of color to Japan's shady groves are one of Japan's classical symbols of the rainy season, which lasts for approximately thirty days every summer. The seasonal beauty of the hydrangeas is accentuated by the gently falling rain that traditionally defined Japan's rainy season. In recent years, however, climate change has led to rain falling in heavy downpours, resulting in the gentle beauty of the vibrant hydrangeas being entirely lost. Climate change is beginning to affect our traditional definitions of the seasons.

Corporate activities are a major factor in climate change, and companies can no longer remain oblivious to the need for environmental conservation. Today, the world faces the contradictory dilemma of needing to secure resources to expand the economy and business, while also needing to protect the environment. In other words, achieving sustainable economic growth is a common concern of contemporary economics faculties, whose traditional subject matter is resource distribution.

Under these circumstances, the value of a corporation is not only defined by its ability to simply generate a profit, but also whether it is sincerely and fully complying with the law. Compliance, however, cannot be ensured simply by stating that the laws and rules must be followed within the company. The very top of the company's management must serve as an umbrella that fosters a corporate culture that eliminates improper conduct on a daily basis. A system must also be established that evaluates the value of a company from a social perspective. When soliciting bids for a project, for example, granting priority to companies that employ people with

The castle town of Matsumae, Hokkaido

disabilities, in addition to offering the necessary technological prowess and price, could serve as a form of practical support to companies making a positive contribution to society.

Because companies are organized to create a profit, honesty and good deeds alone will not lead to a successful business, making efforts to increase profit a necessity. Companies that achieve high profits after overcoming the twin hurdles of environmental conservation and legal compliance can be considered "good companies," and should therefore be valued highly. These companies will then be recognized as increasing their profits by offering the products and services truly needed by their customers.

The practice of regional product rotation employed by the Ohmi merchants, who established themselves throughout all of Japan, served as a source of great wealth. Ohmi merchants began expanding into the cities of Matsumae and Ezashi in Hokkaido starting from the early Edo period. They helped improve techniques to harvest and fish marine products such as kombu seaweed, sea cucumbers, Pacific herring, salmon and Pacific cod, and then exported these products to the Kansai region for use as both food and fertilizer for growing commercial agricultural products such as cotton. They then imported food products, clothing and a variety of daily goods to Hokkaido. To enable the logistics required to operate this product rotation, the Ohmi merchants organized the cargo vessels of Hokuriku into a system of chartered ships.

The regional product rotation method, which combined products produced in distant regions with an efficient system of transport, served to foster the growth of industry in each of the regions, and also disseminate culture to the remote corners of Japan. This helped enhance the quality of life of people in Japan along with generating great wealth for the Ohmi merchants, a clear example of achieving both profitability and corporate value.

6. Enhancing Corporate Governance

The 2003 Group of Eight (G8) Summit was held in the Evian region of France, made famous by the mineral water of the same name. A discussion was held regarding growth in the global economy, leading to the G8 Declaration. Of particular note is the declaration's focus on fostering growth and promoting a responsible market economy, and its call to enhance corporate governance.

The fact that the need to increase the transparency of corporate accounting was discussed in such a forum demonstrates that enhancing corporate governance was seen as the root problem in fostering growth in the global market economy. As demonstrated in the major accounting scandals seen at both Enron and WorldCom in the United States in just the previous year, the uncovering of incidents of accounting fraud can often serve as the lethal blow for companies. In Japan, Resona Bank, one of the country's major financial institutions, had to receive an injection of public funds backed by taxpayers' money on May 17, 2003. It can be said that this was the result of the company's auditor breaking from recent convention and fulfilling its true role as a protector of corporate capital.

In recent years, with cases of automobile manufacturers covering up recalls caused by their own incompetence, false labelling by food manufacturers, and breaches of trust occurring at cleaning goods companies, people have come to question whether corporations themselves have the ability to correct their own behavior. Better corporate governance is greatly needed.

It is natural that companies with powerful influence within society enhance their corporate governance to an even greater degree. Particularly within Japan, there have been many cases where the corporate board of directors, which should serve as the central body in charge of corporate oversight, has not fulfilled its intended duties due to circumstances related to the selection and number of members of the board. To maintain corporate soundness, it is essential that reform of the board of directors and auditing functions be further accelerated, and innovations made to enhance the transparency of management.

Companies that can trace their roots to the Ohmi merchants, which are some of the oldest in the world today, have long incorporated corporate governance into their management systems. The first measure was the forced dismissal process. When the current head of the merchant house was deemed to be engaged in improper activities that could endanger the family assets, guardians, relatives and branch houses would meet for discussion and forcibly dismiss the head of the merchant house if necessary. This was a legitimate process that was clearly set down in the Ohmi merchant house family precepts. The second key measure was the senior manager (*shihainin*) system. As the Ohmi merchants operated numerous branch stores throughout Japan, it was not possible for the head of the merchant house to manage them all directly. To that end, heads would dispatch their very best employees to serve as senior managers of their branch stores. The head would focus on the quality of his employees and finance, and expand his business over a wide territory through a system of delegated responsibility. The third key aspect of corporate governance utilized by the Ohmi merchants was the *tanaoroshi-mokuroku* accounts book, which was produced based on the double-entry accounting principle, and served to aid in the management of branch stores and their senior managers. The senior manager would summarize the key points of management in the store's account book, and submit it to the head of the merchant house. The store account book would be produced according to balance sheet and profit and

The shop accounting book of Nishikawa Jingoro

loss accounting methods, and the profit calculated according to both methods would be reconciled. This served as an effective tool for the head of the merchant house to ascertain the state of management at each of his branch stores.

7. Strength in Technological Development and Creative Innovation

For over twenty years, Japan's GDP has stagnated under poor economic conditions and it was even surpassed by that of China in recent years, with the Japanese economy dropping to third-largest in the world. This led to the perception that Japan's greatest national strength, technological development, was decelerating. When one examines the quality, share of the global market, safety and stability of the highly sophisticated parts and components manufactured within Japan, particularly for the automotive and machinery industries, it is clear that Japan's overall technological strength remains.

Japan's position as an economic superpower is supported by a strength in technological development that was built up over around 150 years. This strength traces its origins to the movement for modernizing Japan, turning it into a country founded on commerce and industry, and improving its technological capabilities, which emerged after the shogunate was threatened by the Western powers. Strength in technological development can be compared to Japan's famous Mt. Fuji. The very leading edge of technological development is supported by a dense foundation of industrial concentration, formed not just of major companies, but by the technological strength of a host of small and medium-sized enterprises (SMEs). Numerous SMEs have devoted themselves to the highly-sophisticated *monozukuri* manufacturing that has become the standard of Japan.

The automotive, multi-function device, and digital still camera sectors, which are leading areas of Japan's manufacturing industry, demand highly sophisticated and precise overall technological strength in the SMEs that make up the component supply chains. The SMEs must possess a wide range of precisely-engineered molds, and make finely-tuned adjustments in the parts they produce. This ecosystem cannot be easily emulated by foreign industries, which is a fundamental strength of the companies that produce the related products and serves as a backdrop to their continued success.

Amidst the unceasing globalization of the world economy, leading companies continue to move their manufacturing bases to low-cost overseas locations, and this has unavoidably led to a reduction in the production volumes of SMEs. This is also, however, the age of IT. Unlike machines and facilities that can be easily moved from one location to another, technological strength, founded on the skills of master craftsmen who devote themselves to daily improvement, ensures that *monozukuri* manufacturing can continue to compete on the global stage, unswayed by the whims of contractors.

The Ohmi merchants, who engaged in a wide range of businesses from fishing to manufacturing and finance, also placed great importance on creative innovation. As typical merchants of the day rarely leveraged their talent to start new businesses, and viewed such ventures with great criticism, the forward thinking of the Ohmi merchants stands out all the more.

In 1893, Okui Mango from Kawanami compared the incredible changes of the day to his experience of walking 1,000 *ri* in a single year, stating, "The West has brought steam ships and railroads, and even the telephone. We can now speak over a distance of 1,000 *ri* and travel 1,000 *ri* in just a day, a feat that would astound even the wrathful deities. Amidst this unbelievable progress, no one can predict the future, and we must strictly devote ourselves daily to tireless innovation to avoid losing to the West."

In Okui's words to his posterity, we can see that he was not blinded by his own achievement in walking

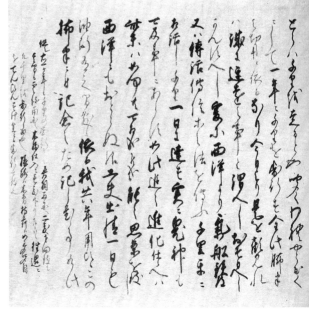

"Memoirs of a 1,000 *ri* Journey" by Okui Mango

1,000 *ri*, and instead soundly perceived the changes seen in society, maintaining a flexible stance that encouraged tireless creative innovation.

8. Innovations in Funding

Without the struggle to obtain funding, there would likely be no more thrilling dream than managing a business. As it is often said, funding is the very lifeblood that sustains a company's daily existence, and the ability to establish an organization that can serve as the beating heart that ceaselessly delivers the necessary funding to a business can determine the success or failure of the venture.

Companies have various goals in seeking funding. They can seek seed funds, operating funds, and forward-looking funds for capital investment, as well as funds that look to the past to cover deficits.

The sources of fund procurement have diversified in line with the astonishing growth of startup ventures seen in 2004. In practical terms, the traditional standard remains acquiring personal financing through funds borrowed from relatives and acquaintances the old-fashioned way, and then using this as a base to secure loans from public financial institutions. Some of the most well-known public financing organizations of the central government include the Japan Finance Corporation (JFC), the Small and Medium Enterprise Unit of the JFC, and the Shoko Chukin Bank. Financing can also be obtained from banks using credit guarantees provided by the Credit Guarantee Corporations of the local metropolitan and prefectural governments.

Although these public financing organizations are stated as providing unsecured and unguaranteed funding, their actual operation differs from what such a description might suggest.

Even if the financing provided

Senryobako, a chest for storing 1,000 *ryo*

by these organizations does not require real estate or financial securities to be offered as collateral, or a third party guarantor, they may apply other conditions. For example, it may require that the company seeking financing join the local Chamber of Commerce and Industry and receive management guidance for a fixed period of time, or require a joint guarantee to be provided by family members or employees to ensure the smooth provisioning of financing. After clearing these requirements, the final hurdle lies in the persuasive power and enthusiasm of the company's officers in securing the understanding of the loan officers while presenting a sound business plan and the relevant documents.

When seeking operating funds for an existing business, it is critical that the managing officers personally understand their business reports, and sincerely present the relevant information to the financial institutions to build a relationship of mutual trust. When viewed on a long-term basis, one time tricks and evasions to secure funding are meaningless, and the only viable path to secure financing are constant efforts to improve a company's finances and sincere efforts to build a relationship of trust with financial institutions through clear disclosure of information.

The Ohmi merchants, who produced numerous renowned merchants over a period of several hundred years, adhered to a policy of maintaining their primary residence in Ohmi Province. Their presence served to inspire the dreams of ambitious young men in the province, and resulted in the creation of countless new businesses that we would call startup ventures today. In other words, the continued presence of successful Ohmi merchants in their hometowns had a positive, demonstrative effect in society.

Ohmi merchants who had already achieved success would provide funding to young people seeking capital to start their own businesses, and offer advice to Ohmi merchants facing difficulties. They did not hesitate to provide operating funds when necessary. When a borrower struggled to make repayments, the Ohmi merchants would rewrite their agreements into a *shusse-shomon*, a simple promise of repayment once the borrower achieved success in the world or improved his financial situation. This financial generosity was a key element in fostering the future generations that would succeed the established Ohmi merchants.

Insights from the Roles of Management

1. The Roles Played by the Merchants' Wives

Whether they were the master or an employee of a merchant house, Ohmi merchants were almost always away from their homes, working at branch stores established in other provinces. Employees who had advanced far enough to be able to marry were able to return home for just fifty days every year, and the master of the merchant house would often be away from home for months at a time, as he travelled among his stores to monitor their management.

Being able to trust that their homes would be well managed and not require support while they were away was a source of strength for the Ohmi merchants. To this end, their wives played a much more important role than that of the typical homemaker at the time. Even the wives of employees played a vital role, raising their children, managing the household accounts, and maintaining friendly relations with the family of the master of the merchant house.

As previously described, after Ito Chubei I became the master of his own merchant house, his wife Yae would not only manage the family affairs, but also take great responsibility for the management of the family trading business. The wives of Ohmi merchants provided lessons in manners to young apprentices who joined their merchant house, and dispatched the new employees to the branch store they were most suitable for, after carefully discerning their abilities and character. The wives also prepared the seasonal uniforms of all the employees, such as their kimonos, *obi* belts, and aprons, and arranged delivery of food supplies to the family's branch stores. At times, they also cared for troubled employees. When employees returned home after making a serious mistake at work, the wives would sit with them at the Buddhist

The wife and children of an Ohmi merchant at home while he is away

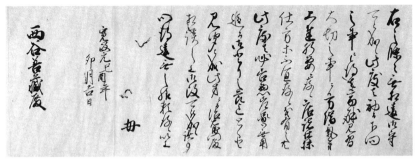

A letter to Nishitani Zenzo from his mother, advising him of his duties as an Ohmi merchant

altar, and provide them with kind teachings and a chance to reflect when the opportunity arose, thus helping them return to employment.

The most important work of the wives of Ohmi merchants, however, was developing the future heirs of their family business, in the event that their husband tragically passed away. One example can be seen in the following letter written in 1789 by the mother of Nishitani Zenzo, the young master of the Nishitani Zenkuro merchant house from Hachiman. The letter contained her teachings for her son as he set out on his first trip to the family's branch store in Yamagata.

"First, you must wake up early, and prepare yourself impeccably, to serve as a model for the employees at the store. Work all day, every day at the store and devote yourself to learning the family business. Treat all the workers who come and go with respect. When you have time, practice writing and the abacus, and occasionally read the writings of the holy men to cultivate yourself. If an apprentice acts improperly, scold him privately, and quickly praise and reward him publicly when he does well. Always make right and wrong clear to him.

When senior employees like the guardian or the store manager disagree with you, the master, quickly accept their words as sincere advice. No matter what happens, always maintain your patience, and even if you are angered, do not allow it to show on your face or in your words. As this is your first visit to a branch store, learning and observing the family business is most important. Even if you see some aspect of the store's management that could be improved, say absolutely nothing and devote yourself wholly to observation. When you return home, discuss what you saw with your advisors, and provide instructions for improvement."

The letter is the embodiment of sense, a demonstration of a mother's true love for a son who had just become the master of a merchant house. It demonstrates how the wives of Ohmi merchants played a key role in developing the human resources of their house, including future heirs. They were not only housewives or mothers, but also vital business partners to their husbands.

2. The *Shiofumi* Training of Young Women

Prosperous Ohmi merchants employed several maidservants at their main residences. Lower-ranked maids (*shimojochu*) worked in the kitchen and looked after the baths and toilets. Upper-ranked maids (*kamijochu*), on the other hand, were not employed as laborers, but rather learned manners by caring for the needs of the master and his wife. Prior to marriage, prominent merchant and farming families would ask Ohmi merchants to take in their daughters as a *kamijochu* for short periods, to teach them the conduct and manners befitting a refined young woman.

Entering the service of a family as a *kamijochu* was known as *shiofumi*, or "stepping on salt." This term was inspired by the perseverance one required to step on salt with bare feet, as even the smallest cut or scrape would bring stinging pain.

During their *shiofumi* service, the young women would learn all the essential skills that a young woman needed to know. This included accompanying the master and his wife when they went out, caring for the family's Buddhist altar, needlework, preparing the seasonal changes of clothing, lessons in tea ceremony and ikebana flower arrangement, and learning the proper behavior and manner of speech to use when going out on errands and the proper greetings to use when they returned. Prosperous Ohmi merchants also received many guests, and sometimes had writers and artists stay at their homes for long periods of time. Learning how to provide hospitality to these guests and

Preparing clothes for the new season

A sewing table and sewing box

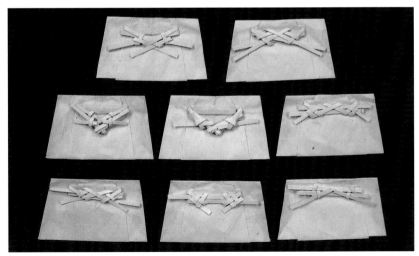

Samples of folded *hakama* pants

participate in refined conversation provided the young *kamijochu* with the ability to judge people.

Nakae Kimi

The 1856 Sahoki household laws established by the Tonomura Yozaemon merchant house from Kondo village stipulated that only the daughters of collateral (*bunke*) or branch (*bekke*) merchant houses could be taken in as *kamijochu*. The family rules further established that *kamijochu* could only marry into branch merchant houses.

Perhaps because the *kamijochu* were primarily engaged in everyday tasks, there are only scant historical records of their activities. The practice of employing young women as *kamijochu* continued until World War II but was rarely seen after that time. Today we can only learn about the practice through interviews with the few remaining people who served as *kamijochu* or witnessed the system personally. In 2009, an interview was held with an 86-year-old woman who, at the age of eighteen, served as a *kamijochu* for two years at the house of Nakae Katsujiro III, one of the most renowned businessmen of his day and the founder of the Minakai Department Store, and his wife Kimi from Kondo. The woman recounted how she primarily studied needlework, and remembered that while she shared the same meals as the master and lady of the house, and was never scolded in any particular way, she still lost ten kilograms simply due to the mental strain, but she gained great perseverance. *Shiofumi* service certainly involved rigorous training.

3. Enjoying Culture

People are naturally attracted to those with an attractive and cultured personality. Ohmi merchants, who overcame the challenges posed by itinerant trading to achieve great success and open many large branch stores, would often host and provide monetary support for purveyors of culture of the day such as artists, authors, Confucian scholars, and haiku poets. Such interaction fostered their personality and breadth as merchants and they came to enjoy themselves a wide range of cultural pursuits, such as the Noh theater, tea ceremony, flower arrangement, the game of Go, *waka* and haiku poetry, and reading and understanding books written in both classical Japanese and Chinese. One illustrative example can be found in the story of Kobayashi Ginjiro (1822–1855), the third generation head of the Kobayashi Chojiya merchant house, who devoted himself to ikebana. Ikebana, the careful arrangement of flowers and greenery as a form of aesthetic

A *rikka* flower arrangement by Ikenobo Senko IV

expression, is one of Japan's original art forms, with a history of over 550 years. Arranging the greenery and flowers in a vase exactly according to one's intentions requires devoted study and practice. While flower arrangement is primarily seen as the pursuit of women today, this was not the case during the Edo period. At the time it was called *kado*, or "the Way of the Flower," and the training of one's spirit was emphasized, encouraging a number of heads of prominent merchant houses to pursue the hobby.

Ginjiro's ties to ikebana started at the age of twenty-two, when he entered the Ikenobo *kado* school. Four years later, he earned the right to present his works at an ikebana exhibition. In another five years, he was considered a master of the art. Today, looking back at the many wood-bound ikebana arrangement books Ginjiro produced during that time, his passionate devotion to the art of ikebana is indisputable.

Among all the hobbies of the Ohmi merchants, landscape gardening and establishing a country retreat would surely have been the most lavish. Through the artistic combination of rocks, ponds, and greenery with the natural landscape, landscape gardens depicted recreations of beautiful natural scenes, for both recreation and aesthetic pleasure. Their popularity spread throughout Japan from the middle of the Edo period. Today, as long ago, creating a landscape garden or building a country retreat requires a significant investment, but Ohmi merchants who had accumulated wealth poured enormous sums into them.

Ichida Yaichiro II, an Ohmi merchant from Kitamachiya in Kanzaki district, started out as an itinerant trader, and went on to achieve success as a merchant of silk, cotton and linen kimonos in the middle of the Meiji period, owning branch stores in Tokyo, Osaka and Kyoto. In 1896, he left his business to his eldest son, and retired to a spacious villa he built on the grounds of Nanzenji in Kyoto. This is Tairyu Sanso, today designated as one of the premier gardens in Japan. Yaichiro utilized a canal running from Lake Biwa to create the ponds in his garden. He also framed

Ichida Yaichiro I

his garden with views of the gentle slopes of the Higashiyama mountains resembling the back of a dragon, and Mt. Hiei and the Kurodani Pagoda at Yoshida-yama can be seen between the trees. The song of the cuckoo can also be heard from time to time.

The Tairyu Sanso villa

Murin-an, the residence Yamagata Aritomo

Ogawa Jihei VII (1860–1933), who devoted himself to landscape gardening, was the foremost garden architect of the Meiji period. Some examples of the many gardens he designed, known collectively as "Ueji's gardens" (Ueji was the title of the head of the Ogawa house), include the garden of the Heian Shrine, and many renowned gardens in the area of the temple of Nanzenji, such as the Seifuso garden of Saionji Kinmochi (1849–1940), a statesman and twice prime minister of Japan, the Hekiunso garden of the Nomura group, and the Yuhoen garden of the Sumitomo group. These are all considered masterpieces of early twentieth-century landscape gardening.

Close to Yaichiro's villa is the Murin-an villa of Yamagata Aritomo (1838–1922), a field marshal, prime minister and privy councillor. One of Japan's most famous landscape gardens, this was where the leaders of the Meiji government gathered and debated Japan's decision to embark on the Russo-Japanese War in 1904. A deep friendship developed between Yaichiro and Aritomo, beyond the simple fact that they happened to be living in villas in the same area with gardens designed by Ueji.

In the autumn of 1904, when Yaichiro turned sixty years old, he and Aritomo exchanged *waka* (poems of thirty-one syllables).

Friends with the pines reflected in the mountain streams, perhaps I will hide myself here for a thousand years—Aritomo

Promising my heart's friend and garden's pines that I will not change for a thousand years—Yaichiro

A fascinating glimpse into the character of the Ohmi merchants is provided by the contrast between their life as merchants, vying for success in trade, and their life after retirement, devoted to elegant artistic pursuits and the enjoyment of the world of arts and culture.

4. The Perspective of Management and Downsizing

I recently received a call from a former student who graduated over twenty years ago, asking to see me. On the day I met him, he showed up in comfortable, stylish clothes. He worked at a department store, and looked to be full of vigor, just shy of turning fifty years old.

His circumstances, however, were far from easy. The first words he spoke to me were, "I just quit my job as part of a downsizing." As part of the third downsizing carried out by his company, he had personally volunteered to be let go. He told me that he could no longer tolerate the grim atmosphere and dropping morale at his company, brought about as staff continuously dwindled throughout the first and second rounds of downsizing. He made his decision seeing no hope for the future at the company. He further told me that he was lucky that his company arranged for him to receive assistance from a recruitment agency, as that safety net was cut away starting from the fourth round of downsizing. I felt I was being shown a vivid picture of the very frontlines of modern society.

The decision to reduce staff through downsizing may be one taken when management is left with no other choices and is at its wits end trying to make its business survive. But looking at the unprecedented scale and frequency of layoffs today, even if such layoffs aid management in helping to return their company to profitability by cutting costs after incurring losses, it is an unavoidable fact that such actions have major long-term implications, such as lowering company morale.

While in the United States it may be accepted as a matter of course that companies will adjust their headcount when the economy or business takes a downturn, this practice is not viewed in the same way in Japan, which is home to a different corporate culture. My former student's story speaks greatly to this fact. The treatment of human resources in business is highly dependent on cultural traditions and values.

Layoffs do not affect only those who lose their jobs, but also those who remain behind, creating a sullen mood in the company. This has led to managers in Japan realizing that layoffs cannot be casually invoked as part of a business restructuring, and has also inspired them to propose new styles of employment based on Japan's cultural traditions, such as competitive lifetime employment. This trend could be considered to be Japan reverting to its natural state.

The Ohmi merchants, who created the *sanpo-yoshi* management philosophy that is still passed down today, placed great importance on considering the long-term impact their business had on society. As can be seen in the following passage, the Kokoroe-sho family precepts laid down in 1856 by the Tonomura Yozaemon merchant house from Kondo warned against pursuing short-term profits simply for personal gain, and stressed the importance of holding a long-term and fair perspective.

> "Our handling of affairs, passed down from long ago, follows the natural law. We never seek victory only for ourselves and we are not swayed by that which is before our eyes. We look out to the distant horizon, and hearken to the unchanging, eternal law."

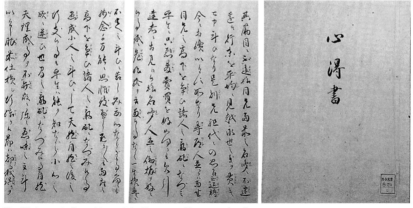

The "Kokoroesho" teachings of the Tonomura Yozaemon family

From the long-term perspective of the Tonomura merchant house, the relationship between management and employees cannot simply be distilled to one of business profit and loss. In Ohmi, the relationship between employers and employees continued until death, through Buddhist rites such as making *segaki* offerings of food and drink to the spirits of former employees, and holding memorial services for employees after they died.

5. The Twilight Years of Founders

When an 85-year-old former prime minister, who had previously been awarded the Order of the Chrysanthemum, the highest honor in Japan, refused to retire in the general election in the autumn of 2003, it provoked a wide debate on the merits and demerits of his choice. While retirement is fundamentally a choice of the individual, the timing of such a choice is always difficult for individuals of great ambition. Entrepreneurs and business founders are no exception.

A business founder who was a pioneer in consumer finance, providing unsecured, small-lot, and instant loans, personally grew his business to the point of being listed on the first section of the Tokyo Stock Exchange, only to be arrested, as the chairman of his company, on wiretapping charges at the age of seventy-three. This may be an extreme example, but the founders of companies in the logistics and restaurant industries have been retiring one after another in recent years against a backdrop of continued poor consumer spending. For example, the founder of a supermarket chain who personally grew his retail business to achieve sales of five trillion yen in the fortieth year after its establishment, a giant in the industry, gave up his position at the age of seventy-eight. Another example can be found in the founder of a hamburger chain, who expanded his business until it ranked first in its industry in Japan in just ten years, and then went on to give up all his positions in the company at the age of seventy-six without even taking an honorary position, before dying disappointed.

These examples leave us with the feeling that while the world is ever-changing, these formerly prominent businesspeople could not discern the changes in consumer trends, and furthermore mistook the timing of their resignation. Due to their strong, self-reliant spirits, founders tend to believe their lives and powers are limitless, and so often become more dictatorial as the years progress.

Moreover, today, in 2004, Japan is the country with the longest lifespans in the world. Men have an average lifespan of 78 years old, and there are many healthy, elderly people.

The relationships between parents and children and husbands and wives, differ today from those in the Edo period. That makes it difficult for the

Honda Soichiro, the founder of the Honda Motor Company

elderly today to enjoy a relaxed leisurely retirement such as that described in *Yojokun* (Life Lessons, 1713) a book by Kaibara Ekiken (1630–1714) a samurai from Fukuoka domain who studied Confucianism and medicine. "Enjoy your days in tranquility, without anger, without greed, and rest your wearied body." In contrast to the aforementioned business founders, Honda Soichiro (1906–1991), the founder of Honda Motors, stated, "If people mistake their landing point, they'll end up losing everything." With his retirement at the age of sixty-six, he serves as a shining example of stepping down at the right time.

The Ohmi merchants, who founded many renowned companies that are still in business today, were nearly all vigorous and long-lived. Niemon, the founder of the Nishikawa Jingoro merchant house from Hachiman, lived to the ripe age of ninety-six years old, and the founder of the Tonomura Yozaemon merchant house from Kondo lived until the age of eighty-four. Kobayashi Ginemon I, from Kotakari in Echi district, lived until seventy-eight years old. He retired at the age of fifty, and fully enjoyed his life after retirement, serving as the village head, and supporting sumo wrestlers in Edo. These men were able to retire with peace of mind because they had developed skilled heirs to take over their business.

Raising or finding an heir they could trust to take over their business was the key to allowing these founders, superlative in both mind and body, to retire in peace.

6. The Failure of Longstanding Businesses and the Quality of Managers

In recent years, many longstanding companies that are both well-known and trusted have been going out of business in quick succession. If one considers companies that have existed for over thirty years to be longstanding, such companies made up ten percent of the companies that went bankrupt in 1994, but ten years later in 2003, that number grew to more than twenty-five percent. When one breaks down the composition by the size of outstanding debts, longstanding companies made up over sixty percent of the medium-sized companies to go bankrupt, with debts between one and ten billion yen.

In general terms, one could say these companies went bankrupt because they could not keep up with changes in their industries, but from a management perspective, it is also a result of them relying too heavily on their goodwill and brand value, and thus growing complacent in their traditional ways of doing business. They had lost the sense of urgency and tension that is necessary to succeed in business.

Today more than ever, the essential qualities of managers, such as decisiveness, foresight, and perseverance, are being tested. Compared to managers in the West, Japanese managers are severely criticized for talking about nothing other than golf and karaoke. Amidst the fierce, unending changes seen today, a company will soon fail if its managers have such a complacent, clueless attitude.

The quality of management plays a particularly decisive role in the fates of small and medium-sized companies (SMEs). Because these qualities cannot be distilled into numbers, they are difficult to discern through financial results. That is why financial institutions, which hold the assets of others, place such great importance on the personal qualities of the presidents of the companies they consider for investment. If the president of a company is seen to lack the determination to personally drive reform and take on new challenges, it is natural that their company will be weeded out.

It is a fact that companies originally founded by Ohmi merchants have also been among those undergoing bankruptcy in recent years. During their long history, however, bankruptcy was not such an unusual occurrence even for the Ohmi merchants.

According to the Zoku-kokenroku treatise, written by Tsukamoto Sadaemon II and recording examples of bankruptcies among the Ohmi merchants around the mid-nineteenth century, most bankruptcies occurred for completely mundane reasons, such as discord within the merchant family, alcoholism, womanizing, a breakdown in store discipline, greed, and indiscretion. All can be traced to an arrogant head of house who had lost control through personal greed.

In 1853, the Ohmi merchant Matsui Yuken, then eighty-three, inscribed on his portrait the words "The proud are doomed to fail." They remain entirely applicable today.

Blaming deflation for the failure of these long-established companies is nothing more than a superficial viewpoint. This is proven by the fact that there are companies in similar businesses that are growing despite the deflationary environment. The greatest difference lies in the quality of their management. To improve their quality, it is essential that managers develop a powerful vision they can share proudly with anyone, while also devoting themselves to realizing that vision daily in their business activities.

Matsui Yuken

7. Developing Human Resources

When I go over the New Year's cards I receive from my former students, I always take an extra moment when I see a note from somebody informing me that they have changed jobs, and I am filled with an earnest wish for their happiness in their new venture. I also worry, however, that it is only those for whom this is a positive development who inform me that they have changed jobs, and wonder if others who may have left their jobs are simply hesitant to inform me of this fact.

Due to changes in the working habits of young people, today, thirty percent we of graduates change or leave their jobs within three years of first entering the workforce. Facing a rapidly aging society, Japan is also expected to see a rapid drop in the number of its young workforce. In light of this, the currently high demand companies have for young workers is not expected to drop any time soon.

Some reasons why young workers have come to change and leave their jobs so frequently include a mismatch between their desires and the reality of the companies they join, or that their lifestyle is not particularly troubled by job-hopping. More extremely, there is now less resistance than ever to being essentially unemployed as a NEET (not in employment, education or training).

It is obvious to anyone that long-term job hoppers and NEETs incur a great burden both to themselves and society. When considering that these individuals will one day want to find regular employment, it is critical that we find ways to reduce the mismatch they find in their job and workplace, and create methods to develop such young workers while reducing their turnover.

Ensuring commonality between the actual management philosophy exhibited by a company's business activities and the value systems of its employees is vital to overcoming this challenge. Fostering such commonality of values will play a major role in encouraging the proactive development of employees and reducing their turnover. That is because everyone, including young people who despise the shackles of society, are in fact seeking a job they can devote themselves to with unequivocal passion.

Ito Chubei I from Hachime, a prominent merchant in the latter half of the nineteenth century who founded both the Itochu and Marubeni general trading companies, was not only a great businessman, but also a great educator. As detailed in Chapter 3, Chubei was a progressive leader who particularly valued freedom and rationality. In the early Meiji period, a time when the former hierarchy of social status still remained in the back of many people's minds, Chubei viewed his employees as important partners, and devoted himself to their development. When he opened his Osaka branch, he included *sukiyaki* in the regular menu, and also held regular *sukiyaki* parties free from hierarchy as a way to foster good relationships and health. He also divided his profits three ways, distributing a portion among his employees, and permitted even young employees to freely voice their opinions in the monthly meetings held at his stores. Furthermore, he encouraged his employees to look beyond only their specific occupations to take a broad view of society. While he was a stately and imposing man, he was also skilled at inspiring his employees to work hard with satisfaction, and deftly drew out the capabilities of young people by promoting them to important positions. Whenever he shared lessons with his employees, he never failed to state that "true freedom is the source of prosperity."

8. Teachings across Three Generations

Today we hear of more cases of child abuse than perhaps any other time in history. These repeated incidents are an indication of an aberration in both families and society. Today is a very difficult time to raise children, as society has undergone a major social change, with extreme importance being placed on respecting individuality. People are becoming more isolated even in the same household or family. Consumer culture also encourages this increasing individualism. With personal computers, smartphones, and home appliances and automobiles packed with microcomputers, we can now easily create an entertaining and comfortable environment entirely in isolation. This same convenience, however, also makes increasing isolation and the dilution of relationships inevitable. Moreover, today we have almost no opportunities to think back and connect with our ancestors on a daily basis.

People, however, can only survive based on their connections to others. There is no denying the ties among family members and relatives. Visiting the graves of one's ancestors, and understanding that we exist thanks to their lives and that we will one day be succeeded by our children, is essential for preventing cases of tragic abuse.

One Ohmi merchant house, that of Tsukamoto Kizaemon from Kondo, made particular use of blood relations when raising future heirs. The founder of the house, Kizaemon III, joined another merchant house in his village at the age of twelve, and worked as an itinerant trader throughout the Hokuriku and Kanto regions. In 1880, he established his own independent house, and seven years later opened his own store, Tsukaki, which sold silk, cotton and linen kimonos in Kyoto. Today, the company is still in the business of kimono-related articles, operating as the Tsukaki Group.

The Kizaemon merchant house has passed down a hanging scroll entitled, "Choja sandai-kagami."

The lowest portion of the scroll depicts a husband and wife working diligently. The middle portion has an illustration of the head of the merchant house treating guests to tea. The uppermost portion illustrates a miserable man with a tattered hat writing frantically with a brush while a dog barks at him. This series of illustrations tells the story of the first generation that toils to achieve success, the luxury of the second generation, and then the failure of the third generation, which knows neither the struggles of founding a business nor the battle to maintain it, and simply fritters its money away on useless extravagance. The lesson of this story is easily understood,

"Choja sandai-kagami"—A view of three generations scroll

even by young children who are just starting to understand the world.

The scroll carries the powerful message that one must never forget the struggles of the founding generation. In instructing children, the second illustration is particularly important. The second generation must have faced its own challenges in maintaining the success of the family business. Indirectly, however, the illustration also suggests that the second generation did not devote itself to educating its children.

When looking at the relationships between father and son and mother and daughter, it is easy for the children to rebel. To prevent such rebellion, it can be helpful to share family teachings starting from a young age as the words of one's grandparents and ancestors, which can encourage children to listen sincerely. To that end, it goes without saying that showing respect to one's ancestors on a daily basis is essential.

Insights from History

1. Merchants and Daimyo Lords

The relationships between politicians and financiers has always been an end-less source of tales throughout the world, whether now or in the past. Ohmi merchants, who expanded their commercial territory throughout Japan, and were seen as some of the wealthiest merchants of their day, had their own share of back-breaking relationships with the daimyo lords of the Edo period. The fate of their merchant houses often hinged on how they managed their relationships with the daimyo, who held absolute power over their domains.

The finances of the daimyo were truly dire from the very inception of their system of rule, and they were constantly in a desperate search for funds. They therefore seized every opportunity and excuse to try and convert the Ohmi merchants, who were outsiders in their lands, into an endless source of funds. The histories of the Nakai Genzaemon and Tonomura Yozaemon merchant houses provide two vivid and contrasting examples of the relationships between Ohmi merchants and the daimyo of the Edo period.

The Nakai Genzaemon merchant house, which saw its Sendai branch store as a particularly irreplaceable treasure chest, had lent a total of 11,825 *ryo* (approximately 600 million yen) to the Sendai domain by 1794. Genzaemon II made repeated attempts to collect the merchant house's loans from the domain, but abandoned his requests when he saw the hopeless state of the domain's finances. In lieu of payments, how-ever, the daimyo granted members of the Nakai house an official family name, and the right to carry swords in the manner of the warrior class.

In the middle of the nineteenth century, in the period before the fall of the shogunate, the Nakai house was obliged to manage the finances of the Sendai domain and serve as its central bank. The domain however, had

Sendai Castle

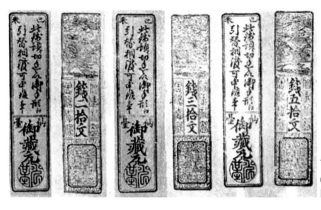

The local Sendai currency issued by the Nakai Merchant House

incurred an astonishing debt of one million *ryo*, and could no longer receive loans from the currency exchangers in Osaka. The Nakai house took up the duty of issuing domain currency and providing loans to foster industry, and by 1858 it had outstanding loans of 250,000 *ryo* to the domain.

In a dire turn of events, however, the Nakai house saw its right to resell Sendai's annual rice tax to Edo unilaterally revoked, ending a source of funds that had served as collateral for the loans it had made. The domain additionally issued an entirely new currency in the same year, causing the value of the previous currency issued by the Nakai to crash, and its name to be hated among the common people. Genzaemon, the fourth head who had struggled to weather these dual challenges, faced forced dismissal (*oshikome-inkyo*) initiated by his employees as the person responsible. Stepping down, he was succeeded by his heir, but the Nakai house never recovered. It had pinned its fortunes on its Sendai branch store, but had no options left when it was faced by the unreasonable demands of the Sendai domain, which manipulated it on the pretense of repaying debts of gratitude to it.

On the other hand, the Tonomura Yozaemon house, whose key location from its beginning had been Nagoya in the Owari domain, was able twice to rebuff invitations from the domain to join the financing organizations it had formed. When the Tonomura declined the second invitation in 1849, it clearly stated that such participation was not appropriate to house custom, and that it was forbidden from joining such organizations by its family reg-

ulations. It was prepared, it said, to be forbidden entry to Nagoya, but warned that such an
action would lead to a decline in trade by other
Ohmi merchants and to a recession in the castle
town. The Tonomura were able to maintain this
strong front against the Owari domain because
its business was not centered solely on Nagoya,
thus benefiting from its regionally-diversified
business strategy.

Nagoya Castle before WWII

2. The Sakuradamon Incident

Ii Naosuke (1815–1860), who suddenly became the thirteenth daimyo of
Hikone domain in December 1850 when his predecessor passed away,
devoted himself to accomplishments by both the pen and the sword from the
time he lived at his family home, prior to succeeding the family name. He
called his residence Umoregi-no-ya, "bog-wood hut," and lost himself in the
secrets of *iai* swordcraft, Zen Buddhism, and the tea ceremony, together with
studying ancient Japanese literature and culture. Naosuke, the very picture of
an enlightened ruler, visited Ohmi in April 1852. At that time, the Kobayashi
Ginemon merchant house, which had branch stores in Edo and Kyoto under
the name Chogin and its main residence in Kotakari, constructed an entirely

new residence to act as a daimyo lodging (*hon-
jin*) for Naosuke, and additionally made a
donation of 2,000 *ryo* to him.

During this period, the shogunate was in turmoil due to the demand by Matthew C. Perry to
open the country to trade. There was a growing
standoff between a faction (Joi) which advocated loyalty to the emperor and the preservation of Japan's isolation and one (Kaikoku)
which supported trade with the West. There
was also at the same time a dispute over who

Ii Naosuke

The Kawara-ban bulletin announcing the Sakuradamon Incident

would succeed as shogun. Naosuke, a member of the Kaikoku faction was involved in a growing rivalry with Tokugawa Nariaki (1800–1860), retired daimyo of Mito, and a member of the Sonno Joi faction. In June 1858, Naosuke was appointed *Tairo*, chief minister of the *bakufu*, and began paying regular visits to the Edo residence of Nabeshima Naomasa, the daimyo of Saga, who was the protector of Nagasaki, and well-informed with regard to international affairs. Influenced by these meetings, Naosuke coolly ascertained the balance of power between Japan and the United States, and signed the Treaty of Amity and Commerce (Harris Treaty) with the United States to avoid war and protect Japan. This unilateral action led Naosuke to order the Ansei Purge (1858–60), in which the chief minister, Ii Naosuke, suppressed those, principally in the Joi faction, that opposed *bakufu* authority. This led to the Sakuradamon Incident.

On March 24, 1860, a frigid snowy morning, Naosuke's entourage was attacked outside the Sakuradamon gate of Edo Castle by eighteen masterless samurai who had illegally left their domains in Mito and Satsuma. Naosuke was killed in the attack. His death greatly undermined the authority of the shogunate in Edo, and

Townsend Harris

served as the turning point toward its final demise.

The Chogin merchant house sent out couriers (*hikyaku*) the same day at 8 pm to inform its Kyoto branch store and the main residence in Kotakari of Naosuke's death. The message, the first intimation of this major incident, contained the cryptic message, "Naosuke's palanquin was surrounded by blades and run through with three longswords, and a war cry of victory was made at that instant." While the fate of Naosuke was uncertain, it was clear that

A *hikyaku* courier

a historic incident had taken place. This confidential information arrived at the Kyoto branch at noon on March 28, just three and a half days after the assassination. Even Hikone domain did not receive the news from its official Edo residence until midnight on March 28, thus illustrating the unprecedented speed at which Chogin's information was disseminated.

The Chogin store in Edo devoted itself to gathering funds for the Hikone domain and loaned it a total of 15,900 *ryo*. At the same time, the Chogin business itself adopted a vigilant posture refraining from transactions, and calling in its accounts due.

Based on their rapid and decisive response to this unprecedented incident, it is clear that the Ohmi merchants possessed a swift information-dissemination network connecting the three major cities of Edo, Kyoto and Osaka, and an organizational structure that responded promptly even in times of crisis. This is no different from the recent past, when the information networks of general trading companies, prepared to respond to incidents around the globe, served as valuable sources of information about major events throughout the world.

3. The Yokohama Gold Rush

A series of treaties, the Ansei Five-Power Treaties, were signed with the

United States in July 1859 (the Harris Treaty) and with four other countries between August and October. They opened Japan to free trade with the West. Merchants who had previously traded exclusively within isolated Japan were suddenly thrown into the dog-eat-dog world of international trade. After the opening of the first three ports, Japan's gold coins were the most heavily-traded item. And while it may have only lasted for a short time, it is possible that as many as one million gold coins left Japan at this time.

As part of the Harris Treaty, the Edo shogunate was forced to accept the equal exchange of foreign currency for domestic currency of the corresponding weight and description. While shogunate officials knew that this would cause a flood of gold currency to leave Japan, they had been forced by Townsend Harris (1804–1878; first U.S. Consul General to Japan), the U.S. negotiator, to accept the currency clause in exchange for restrictions on the free passage of foreigners throughout Japan. These restrictions served to protect Japan's fledgling industries from powerful foreign investment, and greatly contributed to the country's economic growth after 1868.

Japan's method of determining the exchange rate between gold and silver coins greatly differed from international standards, and this was a direct cause of the large outflows of gold currency during this period. At the time, one *ryo* of gold (the *tempo-koban* gold coin) could be exchanged for four *tempo-ichibugin* silver coins. The *tempo-ichibugin* were, however, a subsidized currency with a value three times greater than their actual weight in silver. Furthermore, while in terms of weight, one U.S. silver dollar (also referred to as a "Mexican dollar") was equivalent to three *tempo-ichibugin*, in terms of currency value, it was only equivalent to one *tempo-ichibugin*. However, in accordance with the Harris Treaty, the exchange standard was based solely on weight, meaning that one U.S. silver dollar could be exchanged for three *tempo-ichibugin* silver coins. Therefore, if you exchanged one silver dollar in Japan for *tempo-ichibugin*, you could leave the country with three times what you started out with by currency value. For example, if you brought four silver dollars into Japan, you could exchange them for 12 *tempo-ichibugin*. These could then be exchanged for three *ryo* of gold. When brought abroad, these three *ryo* would be the equivalent of 12 silver dollars, meaning you would have tripled your money.

Foreign merchants thus competed fiercely to purchase as much Japanese currency as they could, leading to a sharp rise in domestic exchange rates for gold coins, which enticed the Ohmi merchants, who were always deeply interested in utilizing their excess reserves, into the world of currency speculation.

Tempo-koban, tempo-ichibugin, and silver one dollar coin

The Kobayashi Ginemon house, which had branch stores in Edo and Kyoto under the name of Chogin, primarily bought its currency in the Kyoto and Osaka region, and held it at its Edo branch. The Chogin currency merchants were known as *kinkata* (asset managers) and they primarily purchased *tempo-koban* gold coins, *tempo-ichibukin* gold coins, *tempo-nishukin* gold coins, and U.S. silver dollar coins.

Chogin, which was well-informed on internal affairs through Utsugi Rokunojo (1809–1862) of the Hikone domain, the official who managed affairs with the shogunate for Ii Naosuke, purchased currency at a fevered pitch throughout the six months immediately after the opening of Japan's ports, with a particular focus on gold. By the beginning of 1860, the house had accumulated the equivalent of 8,857 *ryo* in *tempo-koban* gold coins and 2,165 *ryo* in *tempo-ichibuban* gold coins. On February 11 the same year, the shogunate issued a currency exchange order of 3.37 times for 100 *ryo* of *tempo-koban* gold coins and 3.25 times for 100 *ryo* of *tempo-ichibuban* gold coins to stop the outflow of currency. As a result, Chogin saw a surplus marginal gain of 25,906 *ryo*, and the assets of its Edo store rose to 53,155 *ryo*, double that of the previous year.

The opening of Japan's ports led to a gold rush that originated in Yokohama and to a domestic bubble. By issuing currency exchange orders that only addressed gold coins, the Shogunate caused severe inflation to occur, and this spurred great turmoil at the end of the Edo period.

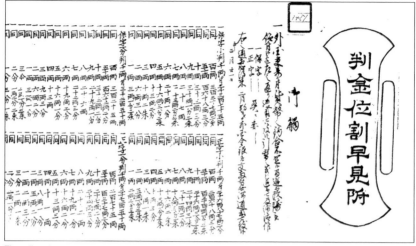

The edict of raising the value of gold coins

4. The Bankruptcy of a Currency Exchanger

On the morning of December 8, 1861, the Kyoto currency exchanger Iseya Tobei, popularly known as Iseto, suddenly went bankrupt. Iseto was a prominent currency exchanger and one that served the Kyoto municipal administration (*Kyoto machibugyosho*). He even had his own branch store in Edo. His bankruptcy was caused by the speculative trading in gold and silver coins that accompanied the opening of Japan's ports.

Iseto had a total of 211 clients when he went bankrupt, concentrated in neighboring provinces of Kyoto such as Yamashiro, Ohmi, Tanba, Tango and Osaka. They also spread even further along the Tokai region as far as Mino and Owari provinces. His creditors included currency exchangers from Kyoto and Osaka, saffron dye and silk wholesalers in Kyoto, and the residences maintained by daimyo in Kyoto, as well as temples and Kyoto aristocrats. Iseto's largest clients though were the Ohmi merchants.

Of the 576,000 *ryo* of debt Iseto owed, 330,000 *ryo* was owed to 43 Ohmi merchant clients. Kobayashi Ginemon was his largest creditor, who was owed 138,000 *ryo*, followed by Matsui Kyuemon, who was owed 98,000 *ryo*. Other prominent Ohmi merchants included Koizumi Shinsuke, Tonomura

Yozaemon, Abe Ichirobei, Fujii Zensuke and Takada Zenemon.

With the bankruptcy of Iseto, who had effectively served as a central bank, there were growing fears that there would be a crisis of management in the Kobayashi Ginemon merchant house (Chogin), which was a large creditor of Iseto. Chogin responded by continuing to exchange currency through other currency exchangers, temporarily halting exchanges at its Kyoto and Osaka branches, and transferring surplus funds from its Edo branch to Kyoto and Osaka. As a result, on December 24, 1861, Chogin, which devoted itself to maintaining external trust, closed its Osaka money exchange, which had only opened that March.

Spearheading the response to this crisis was Ginemon II, then sixty-two. When he decided to close the Osaka branch, Ginemon addressed his employees, who were bitter about what they felt was Iseto's betrayal.

"During such a crisis, what is most important is not to be constrained by the short-term reputation of the house, but rather for everyone to attend scrupulously to what happens next, even if it means reducing business competition." Ginemon explained that if they focused on making a good external impression, they would not be constrained in their future transactions. He explained that while he had encountered many unexpected calamities since his childhood, as long as he responded carefully, business always recovered naturally and expanded even further. Ginemon thus made a compelling explanation to his employees of the importance of following up on an unprecedented crisis, based on his own experiences, in the manner of the old adage, "an ill bird fouls its own nest."

For Chogin, which had just had a major commercial success in gold currency exchange the previous year, the events of 1861 represented a major drawback. It was able to survive the crisis, however, through the rapid and calm response of Ginemon II, and recovered its position as a prosperous merchant house post 1868. Ginemon II was clearly a man who followed through on his own words with action.

Kobayashi Ginemon II

5. The Tenchu Panic

Political unrest reached its climax between 1861 and 1863. Under the leadership of the Kobu Gattai faction, which sought to achieve stability in Japan through union between the imperial court in Kyoto (Ko) and the shogunate in Edo (Bu), major problems and incidents occurred one after another. One was opposition to the proposed marriage of Princess Kazunomiya, the younger sister of Emperor Komei, to the shogun, Tokugawa Iemochi. A second was the Namamugi Incident in which four British subjects were attacked by Satsuma bodyguards for not dismounting to let the retinue of Shimazu Hisamitsu, regent of the Satsuma daimyo, pass. This resulted a year later in the so-called Anglo-Satsuma War. On June 25, 1863, Choshu domain forces fired on foreign ships passing through the Straits of Shimonoseki, against shogunate orders. Then on September 30, 1863, the Kobu Gattai faction, led by the Satsuma and Aizu domains, expelled from Kyoto the Sonno Joi (literally, "Revere the Emperor, Expel the Barbarians") faction, led by the Choshu domain, which had demanded that Emperor Komei announce the expulsion of all foreigners. The conflict between the two factions continued, attended by unabated unrest.

During this period, the Sonno Joi faction made appeals to urban residents suffering from rising prices due to the opening of Japan's ports, and accused currency exchangers, rice merchants and merchants engaged in foreign trade, vigorously putting up posters in public places and throwing anonymous letters into merchants' houses. Merchants engaged in foreign trade were particularly

Kanagawa (Yokohama) after the opening of foreign trade

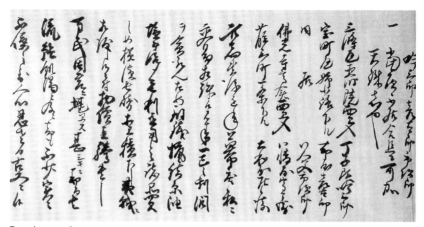

Terrorism warning

targeted by frequent acts of terrorism, as it was assumed that these merchants raised prices by cornering the market and restricting sales to gain unreasonable profits. Such violence was justified as the vengeance of heaven (*tenchu*).

Early in the morning of September 5, 1863, a poster was put up anonymously on the notice board at the edge of the Great Sanjo Bridge (Sanjo Ohashi) in Kyoto, predicting heaven's vengeance upon Chojiya Ginzaburo, Nunoya Hikotaro and his father Ichijiro, Yawataya Ubei, and Yamatoya Shobei.

> "Since the shogunate unilaterally opened Japan's ports, these people have traded only for their personal profits and sold valuable goods and daily necessities to foreign countries in Nagasaki and Yokohama, causing these supplies to grow increasingly scarce and prices to rise. As a result, the lives of ordinary people are tremendously difficult, and we can no longer look upon these people dispassionately. Therefore, we shall mete out the vengeance of heaven upon the listed individuals on behalf of the nation, and display their heads to the public."

That night, just Yawataya Ubei was killed, and his severed head was exposed on the Sanjo Bridge the next day, September 6. The criminal declaration posted below Ubei's head stated that the remaining four individuals, who could not be found the previous night, would be tracked down and killed. Chojiya Ginzaburo was however simply the name of the Kyoto branch of the Kobayashi Ginemon Chojiya merchant house, which was commonly referred to as Chogin. That night, five masterless samurai broke into the store and caused the equivalent of 500 *ryo* in damage while they were searching for the non-existent Chojiya Ginzaburo, whom they thought to be an actual person.

The following week, members of the Chogin store, seeking to save Ginzaburo from assassination, put up a poster on the Sanjo Bridge stating their contrition for engaging in foreign trade in the confused pursuit of profit. However there was no response and the fear of assassination continued.

In consideration of the trouble this disturbance caused the neighborhood, the Chogin store was eventually forced to close temporarily. While looking for another location for a temporary store, its members continued making appeals in various directions to save Ginzaburo and to resume business at the original store. They eventually called upon the Choshu domain's Kyoto residence and went on to donate 10,000 *ryo* to the Gakushuin political association, which was identified with the Choshu domain.

They delivered the 10,000 *ryo* to the Choshu domain's residence on September 30, the very day of the attempted coup d'état by the Sonno Joi faction. Despite this payment, it was still not possible to reopen the Kyoto branch at its original location, and after the death of the senior manager due to illness, the staff finally changed the name of their temporary shop to reopen for business in July 1867.

The turmoil surrounding the fall of the shogunate caused terrible strife for merchants, who were always forced to operate within the sociopolitical structure of the time. The merchants were subjected to irrational terrorism, and were also caught in a constant struggle to find saviors and forced to donate large sums of money. This was truly a tumultuous period.

6. Ocean Voyages of the Meiji Period

Though extremely successful during the Edo period, the Ohmi merchants have tended to be viewed as anachronisms in decline once the Meiji period

(1868–1911) began. It is thus extremely rare to hear stories about their exploits after that time.

This perspective, however, must be reviewed based on historical fact. According to a gazetteer of the districts of Gamo, Kanzaki and Echi in Shiga Prefecture compiled in the 1920s, a survey of branch stores, including those overseas, opened by Ohmi merchants shows that 541 shops were opened in the Meiji period, and 412 shops were opened in the Taisho period (1912–1926). Furthermore, a petition conducted among residents of Shiga Prefecture in 1892 to press for the construction of a railway station at Kawase on the Tokaido railway line that ran along the eastern shore of Lake Biwa between Notogawa and Hikone emphasized that there were 1,965 merchants who would use the station to trade outside the prefecture. The petition would go on to succeed, with the construction of the new station taking place as requested. The activities of the Ohmi merchants had clearly become even more vigorous since the start of the Meiji period.

All merchants, not only Ohmi merchants, were forced to deal with the massive transformation brought about in the twenty or so years after 1868 and many felt bewildered and ended up swept along by the dictates of the times. The Revolution of 1868 was first and foremost one of political reform, and the common people, including merchants, could only play a secondary role. Prosperous merchants in particular were in a passive position, used only as a source of funds.

Matsukata Masayoshi (1835–1924), who became the Minister of Finance as part of the political changes of 1881, implemented a deflationary financial policy over a long period as a means of financial reform. Merchants, feeling their family businesses had reached a deadlock, for the first time made voluntary moves to break the impasse. Their financial strength and activities may be said to have provided the springboard for the industrial revitalization that began around 1886.

Matsukata Masayoshi

Among Ohmi merchants, Kobayashi Ginemon IV and Abe Ichisaburo both traveled themselves to the West in 1887 to purchase textile machinery. Ginemon set out from Yokohama on April 24, and traveled to Britain by way of San Francisco, Chicago and New York, ordering two hundred looms in Manchester. He went on to travel through Europe, visiting France, Germany and Italy. He returned to Japan from Marseilles and called at Alexandria, Colombo, Singapore and Hong Kong before arriving in Yokohama on November 8. In this epic half-

Kobayashi Ginemon IV

year ocean voyage around the world, we can see Ginemon's powerful spirit and ambition. The looms were installed at the Onagigawa Cotton Textile Company (now Fujibo Holdings, Inc.), of which Ginemon merchant was the largest shareholder.

The same vigor can be seen in the new initiatives undertaken by other merchants. In 1888, the Abe merchant house founded the Kanakin Weaving Company (now Toyobo Co., Ltd.), and in 1889, Hirose Sukesaburo from Hikone founded the Nippon Life Insurance Company, which would go on to become one of the largest life insurance companies in the world. In 1894, powerful Ohmi merchants such as Koizumi Shinsuke VII and Ito Chubei I jointly founded the Ohmi Bank, and in 1895, former samurai from Hikone domain and Ohmi merchants from Koto pooled their resources to establish the Ohmi Railway Company.

While some of these new business ventures succeeded, others

Invoice for textile machinery

of course failed. Their success and failure illustrate that business is a living being in any age, and that managers must constantly be attuned to changes both within and without, always ready to respond.

7. Branch Stores on the Asian Continent

In recent years (2004) we have seen the active expansion of Japanese companies into China. With a rapidly growing economy bolstered by a vast territory and a massive population, it is natural that China would have strong appeal as both a production base and as a market. The expansion of Japanese companies into the Asian continent, including both China and the Korean Peninsula, is no recent affair. Japanese merchants began opening stores in China in the early Meiji period. One early entrant to the Chinese market was the Minakai Department Store chain, founded by the Ohmi merchant Nakae Katsujiro III (1872–1944).

Katsujiro was the eldest son born to the Nakae merchant family of Kondo, which traded in clothing and sundry goods. At the age of fifteen, he began itinerant trading in Ise, Mino and Owari in the Tokai region to learn the family's clothing trade. He took over the family business in 1897 and opened his first branch store in Daegu in Korea in 1905. In 1911, he moved his main clothing store to Keijo (now Seoul), and from 1913 to 1919, opened additional branch stores in Wonsan, Busan, and Pyongyang. In 1922, Katsujiro consolidated his various branch stores into a company called the Minakai Clothing Store with seed capital of two million yen, where he served as president. The headquarters of his company was his own main residence in Kondo.

In June 1924, Katsujiro set off on a three-month trip through the United States, Mexico and Canada to observe the state of business there. Koizumi Jusuke III (1878–1945) and Koizumi Seizo were his travel companions. Jusuke, who ran a clothing wholesale business in Bingo-machi in Osaka, hailed from the village of Asahi and so was a close neighbor of Katsujiro, while Seizo, who had studied at Columbia University in New York, served as both translator and guide. During his tour of the United States, Katsujiro was keenly aware of the wealth and power of the emerging industrialized nation,

Memorial photograph of the ocean voyage
to North America: From the right, Jusuke,
Katsujiro and Seizo

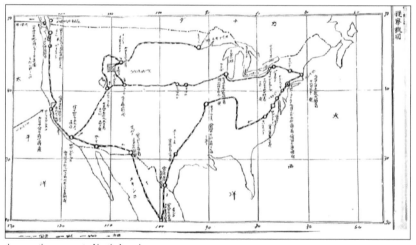

Journey the voyage to North America

blessed with a broad natural environment, abundant resources, and rapidly
becoming a motorized society. At the same time, however, he also became
aware of the harsh prejudice against Japanese immigrants in the United States.

The knowledge they gained on their tour of North America motivated
Jusuke and Katsujiro regarding their future expansion in the clothing business. Jusuke, the wholesaler, placed great importance on developing new,
proprietary products under the motto of "special, distinctive products," and
based himself in Osaka. He went on to found the Koizumi Group, which

Map of Minakai and Chojiya shops in Northeast Asia

today includes the Koizumi Corporation, the Koizumi Sangyo Corporation, and the Koizumi Seiki Corporation. Katsujiro transformed his Minakai Clothing Store on the Asian continent into a department store chain. He was particularly successful in expanding throughout the continent, and by 1938, he had, directly or through affiliated companies, opened stores in Seoul, Busan, Daegu, Pyongyang, Hamhung, Wonsan, Gunsan, Mokpo, Daejeon, Gwangju, Kiitsu, Fun Nam, and Jinju in Korea, and Xinjing (now Changchun), Fengtian (now Shenyang), Harbin and Beijing in China.

Minakai was not the only department store founded by an Ohmi merchant to expand into the Asian continent. Kobayashi Genroku (1867–1940), a relative of the Kobayashi Ginemon merchant house, opened a Western garment store called Chojiya in Tsu in Mie Prefecture, and went on to open branches in Busan and Seoul in 1904, and even in Vladivostok in Russia. Genroku incorporated Chojiya as a stock-based entity in 1921, and transformed his shops into department stores. He also opened additional stores in Changchun, Shenyang, Dalian, Pyongyang, and Wonsan.

The expansionist trajectory of the Minakai and Chojiya department stores was cut off with Japan's surrender on August 15, 1945. It is a timeless fact that international affairs play a large role in the success and failure of business activities abroad.

8. Immigrants from Koto in Canada

There are likely few people today, even in Shiga Prefecture itself, who know that there is a region known as the "Immigrant's Village" in the Koto area. From the 1890s to 1930s, many village people, centered around Hassaka in Hikone, where the Shiga Prefectural University is now located, set off across the ocean to Canada. In a survey of Japanese expatriates conducted in Canada before World War II, individuals from Shiga Prefecture made up the greatest portion of Japanese immigrants. According to the Canadian national census of 1920, Japanese originally from Shiga Prefecture made up 3,054 people of the total of 17,475 Japanese nationals residing in Canada, the highest number from any individual prefecture. Among the immigrants from Shiga, over half were from villages in Inukami district, near the eastern shore of Lake Biwa.

Until the early Meiji period, farmers in these villages supplemented their income by means of linen production, as well as peddling and taking up apprenticeships all over Japan. After 1868, they vigorously expanded their business activities outside the prefecture. Once people knew that the ground-work to go overseas was sufficiently in place, migration to Canada became a new alternative to realizing their dreams of getting rich quickly, in addition to the previous options of peddling or working for a merchant house.

The rising water line of Lake Biwa imparted further momentum to the migration of Shiga Prefecture villagers to Canada, which started in earnest from around 1890. Lake Biwa rose to a record level in 1896, even reaching Buddhist altars in people's homes. The enormous damage caused by the flooding resulted in the sharp rise in the number of migrants to Canada. The immigrants sent back large sums of money to aid their families in Japan.

The Matsumiya Shop on Powell Street

One family account book recorded that 105 yen was sent back over the course of a year in 1899 by a relative from Kaideima in Hikone who had migrated to Canada. At that time, one would have to work for over ten years as the employee of a merchant house to earn an annual salary over 100 yen. Migrating to Canada allowed people to send home a sum equivalent to the pay of a ten-year veteran in a merchant house.

A wide range of individuals migrated to Canada, including Matsumiya Sotojiro from Kaideima, who had previously served as an apprentice of a clothing merchant, and Kitamura Sukezaemon from Hikone, who abandoned his apprenticeship at a clothing shop.

After making his first trip to Canada in 1905 at the age of trenty-three, Matsumiya opened a Japanese-Western sundry goods and grocery store on Powell Street in Vancouver, a popular neighborhood for Japanese residents, while continuing to travel back and forth between Canada and Japan. Most Japanese immigrants, however, could not understand English, and so first worked as laborers at sawmills and fish canning factories. People who worked hard like Kitamura Sukezaemon to learn English at night school advanced to work at jobs such as a bellboy at a hotel, and thus started saving money to live on. Sukezaemon would go on to open a pharmacy and sundry goods shop named Taishodo on Powell Street in Vancouver.

Kitagawa Genzo from Kaideima and Kuwahara Sataro from Hikone serve as examples of individuals who succeeded in starting their own businesses despite struggling with discrimination and prejudice after migrating to Canada. The two opened a shop selling silk textiles and women's clothing made in Japan. The store employed and served local Canadian residents.

The two businessmen managed to struggle through World War II, and

The founders of SILK-O-LINA CO. From the right: The SILK-O-LINA CO. shop
Shigejiro, Genzo, and Sataro

succeeded in growing their business into a company called Silk-O-Lina which they managed jointly and which consisted of a chain of eighteen shops throughout central and western Canada. While Kuwahara, the president of the company, passed away in 1953 at the age of sixty-six, Kitagawa was the first Japanese person to be awarded the Order of Canada at the age of seventy-six in 1973, in recognition of the contribution he and Kuwahara had made to the local community.

These business ventures, undertaken by migrants who crossed the Pacific Ocean to start their businesses in foreign lands, demonstrate the true worth of the Ohmi merchants, individuals with daring and undaunted spirits, and a unique and expansive worldview.

FINAL CHAPTER

Contributing to Society through Anonymous Good Deeds

Nakai Genzaemon I

The Legacy of Nakai Genzaemon I

Ohmi merchants who succeeded in building their assets through itinerant trading and expanding their commercial territory across all of Japan next turned their attention to ensuring the perpetuity of both their family and business. Modern Japan's emphasis on perpetuity over profit can be traced to this practice. The Ohmi merchants concluded that doing good deeds in the world without making their name known, in other words anonymous good deeds, was the only way to achieve their goal of a long-lasting family business.

Nakai Genzaemon I (1716–1805) lost both his parents at a young age, and set out to the Kanto region as a travelling medicine merchant in 1734 at the age of nineteen. He started his business with a total of 20 *ryo* of seed capital, the combination of 2 *ryo* of personal capital combined with 18 *ryo* borrowed from his uncle. Genzaemon made repeated peddling trips between Ohmi and the Kanto regions, and incorporated products such as textiles into his line-up to further increase his revenue. By 1769, he had accumulated net assets of 7,468 *ryo*, and established a branch store in Sendai, over 800 kilometers from his home in Ohmi. He then further expanded his business by establishing a complementary network of stores in eastern Japan and the urban regions around Kyoto and Osaka. He began carrying out regional product rotation, the business model that serves as the prototype of modern *sogo shosha* (general trading companies), rotating products such as raw silk and used clothing between the two regions. Genzaemon soon became one of the renowned Ohmi merchants of his day. In 1804, the year before his death, the Nakai merchant house had succeeded in building over 115,375 *ryo* of net assets. Genzaemon was truly one of the leading Ohmi merchants, who set himself a firm life goal and succeeded through tireless work.

The phrase "anonymous good deeds" also appears in the written work *Kanemochi Shonin Ichimai Kishomon* (One Sheet Vow of a Wealthy Merchant), which recorded Genzaemon's secret teachings about becoming a wealthy merchant. It was something to which he attributed the greatest importance. According to Genzaemon, wealthy people could be divided into two categories, ordinary wealthy people and wealthy people called *choja*, who represented their entire province. Genzaemon asserted that becoming an ordinary wealthy merchant with assets from 50,000 to 100,000 *ryo* was not a matter of luck. Anyone could become ordinarily wealthy if they were good people who suppressed their desires, conquered the distractions of feasting, idle pleasure and luxury, and earnestly devoted themselves to sustainability, frugality and diligent work. Genzaemon further explained that becoming a great *choja* was impossible in the first generation, and one must be blessed with heirs in the second and third generation who are good people that aspire to join the ranks of the ordinarily wealthy. Whether a merchant house could succeed in repeatedly producing good heirs, however, was essentially a matter of fate. According to Genzaemon, to elicit the good fortune necessary to be blessed with good heirs, one can only pray while carrying out anonymous good deeds.

Genzaemon cited anonymous good deeds as the only way to invite good fortune, which was always capricious and fleeting, and to be blessed with a good heir. He further explained that in

Kanemochi Shonin Ichimai Kishomon

order to perform anonymous good deeds, one's mind cannot be consumed by frugality and stinginess. He asserted that the anonymous good deed of sharing legitimately-earned profits for use in community service could also be considered an aspect of frugality, as it results in the efficient use of live capital, and that one must not be overtaken by the miserly tendency to look only at short-term profit and loss. Genzaemon explained that frugality and stinginess are mindsets of the consumer, and that if one did not understand that the righteous path is positioned in exactly the opposite direction from these tendencies, it would be impossible to perform anonymous good deeds and pray for a good heir.

The anonymous good deeds that symbolized Genzaemon's philosophy included a wide range of acts, such as donating rice and money, paying the annual rice tax for those who could not afford it, extending the repayment period or exempting borrowers from paying back their loans, making donations to shrines and temples, undertaking construction to create employment, improving bridges and roads, improving irrigation systems, managing water usage, improving mountains and riversides, and donating to education. While these acts could, in essence, be considered part of economic and social policy, which was the responsibility of the government, individual Ohmi merchants undertook these burdens personally as a form of social contribution. Even when these deeds were initially performed as virtuous acts known by everyone, it was inevitable that they would eventually become anonymous good deeds with the passing of time.

The *sanpo-yoshi* philosophy of the Ohmi merchants serves as the origin for their practice of performing anonymous good deeds to ensure the sustainability of their family businesses. *Sanpo-yoshi* discards the notion that the sustainability of a business can be ensured simply by making money, and asserts that trade should constantly be carried out with a focus on contributing to society as a whole, and not solely for the purpose of generating profit. While the exact number of anonymous good deeds performed by the Ohmi merchants is unknowable, it is possible to present a selection of examples drawn from the long-established companies that were founded by Ohmi merchants and are still in operation today.

Donating Rice and Money

The Yao Kihei merchant house was founded in 1749, and primarily operated department stores and breweries. The year 2018 marked the 270th anniversary of these longstanding companies. After becoming independent at the age of thirty-nine from the merchant house he had joined as an apprentice, Kihei I opened a brewery and general trading store in the Chichibu region of Saitama Prefecture, 500 kilometers away from his home in Ohmi, starting his business with seed capital of 120 *ryo* as a 50–50 *noriai-akinai* joint venture launched together with his original merchant house. The Chichibu region served as the focal point of Kihei's business, and he opened a network of sixteen stores. The Yao merchant house always took pains to maintain good relationships with the villages in the areas where it opened stores. At the Chichibu branch shop, senior staff members would make their way from the center of the town all the way to the outskirts to offer New Year's greetings on January 2. They would make additional rounds of greetings in the same manner on the festival days of March 3, May 5, July 7 and September 9. During the Chichibu Festival held in November, the shop would offer a feast to visitors.

In addition to constantly performing these virtuous deeds, the Yao merchant house also donated rice and money in extraordinary circumstances. During times of famine or bad harvests, its stores would make donations of rice and money to the local people as quickly as possible, and sell additional rice at a low cost. The stores would also distribute rice on memorial days for former heads of the house, and when the current head passed away. Even after the branch store had been open for one hundred years, Yao Kihei IV, who was a keen student of *Sekimon*, cautioned his employees, who were all from Ohmi province, never to lose their consciousness of being outsiders (*yosomo-*

The clothes worn by Yao Kihei I during his days as a traveling merchant

no-ishiki) and always hold themselves to the highest standards of conduct.

There was even a time when this form of management, considerate of the local people and region, managed to save the Chichibu shop. In 1884, Chichibu farmers banded together in an armed uprising known as the Chichibu Incident. That year marked the very

The Chichibu Incident

peak of the economic depression brought about by the deflationary policies of Finance Minister Matsukata Masayoshi to address the issue of unexchangeable currencies. After Japan opened itself up to free trade with the West in 1859, the Chichibu region was drawn into the monetary economy as it was a region exporting raw silk, and its farmers suffered under merciless usury. When the local government rejected the request from the Chichibu farmers to extend their loan repayment dates, they joined forces with a radical political party in an armed uprising, and took control of the Chichibu region for one week.

At that time, the Chichibu branch was already the preeminent merchant store in the Chichibu region. In such a crisis, one would expect that, being run by outsiders from Ohmi, the store would have been the first establishment to be targeted. However, the members of the uprising did not raid it, recognizing that it was not the sort of shop that engaged in unjust business such as usury, and so guaranteed its normal operations. They even asked the shop staff to cook the rice for their troops. However, places seen as responsible for oppressing the people, such as usurers, the local government office and the police station were burned down. Even in the tumultuous environment of an armed uprising, the business practices of the Chichibu branch, conscious of its being a stranger in a distant land, were highly regarded by the rebels.

Improving Mountains and Riversides

Tsukamoto Corporation Co., Ltd., which is today listed on the First Section of the Tokyo Stock Exchange, traces its origins to the branch store opened in

Kofu, (present Yamanashi Prefecture) by Tsukamoto Sadaemon I in 1812. He began itinerant trading in eastern Japan in 1807 at the age of nineteen, dealing in *komachi-beni* (premium lipstick) and a limited amount of linen textiles, with initial seed capital of 5 *ryo*. After surveying the market for a period of five years,

From the right: Tsukamoto Sadaji II and Masayuki

Sadaemon chose to open his first branch store in Kofu. He went on to open an additional branch store in Kyoto in 1839 to procure silk clothing. Sadaemon II took over the family business in 1851, and, together with his younger brother Masayuki, further expanded the business founded by their father. After the new Meiji government was established in 1868, the two brothers formulated a commercial policy for the new age entitled "Tsukamoto Moshiawase-sho." They then expanded the business yet again, opening a store in Tokyo in 1872, and founding the Tsukamoto Gomei Corporation in 1893.

Sadaemon II and Masayuki did not balk at spending money for public construction work, road works, donations to disaster victims, or forestry projects. Of the many acts of philanthropy by the Tsukamoto merchant house, the most noteworthy is undoubtedly its donation for the improvement of the mountains and riversides around Lake Biwa to prevent the accumulation of sediment, a project that demonstrated foresight that extended one hundred years into the future. This philanthropic project was carried out with supporting funds from the Shiga prefectural government, and over a period of fourteen years, starting from 1894, dams were constructed and saplings planted over an area of 2.6 square kilometers. The construction costs of 57,000 yen were divided in a two-to-one split between the prefectural government and the Tsukamoto merchant house.

They funded one more prominent project to improve mountains and riversides. Kofu, the home of the first branch store of the merchant house, suffered devastating damage from torrential rain in 1907 and 1910. In 1911, in response to the damage caused by flooding, Emperor Meiji bestowed 3,000 square kilometers of imperial forest located upstream of the rivers flowing into Kofu to the Yamanashi prefectural government. That very same year, the Tsukamoto house established the Tsukamoto Gomei Corporation and also celebrated the centenary of when Tsukamoto Sadaemon I began itinerant trading. In recognition of the terrible damage suffered by the region housing their first branch store, the Tsukamoto made a donation of 10,000 yen to the Yamanashi prefectural government to support planting trees. The prefectural government decided to use this money

Memorial statue on Mt. Tsukamoto

to support the cost of planting trees to prevent flood damage in the prefectural forests newly bestowed by the Emperor, and named a portion of the forest Mt. Tsukamoto in honor of the family. Over a period of two years, Japanese cypress and cedar saplings were planted there. Since that time, Mt. Tsukamoto has been continuously cared for through weed clearing and tree pruning, and, as a result, is a beautiful forest that produces timber of exquisite quality today. One can still find a monument to the Tsukamoto Gomei Corporation quietly standing in the forest, unnoticed even by the citizens of Kofu.

Donating an Elementary School

Furukawa Tetsujiro (1878–1940) was born in Toyosato in Inukami district, and joined the merchant house of his uncle-in-law, Ito Chubei I, as an apprentice at the age of twelve. As Chubei's right-hand man, Tetsujiro advanced through the ranks steadily, and learned accounting. In response to the great depression that occurred after World War I, the stores of Chubei and his elder brother Chobei

Furukawa Tetsujiro during his days as Executive Director

merged in 1921 to form the textile wholesaler Marubeni Corporation. This would grow into the *sogo shosha* Marubeni Corporation, which is today known throughout the world. Both the president and vice-president were from the same family, and did not involve themselves in the management of the company. Tetsujiro, who was endowed with the spirit of entrepreneurship and a resolute personality, became the executive director of Marubeni at the age of forty-four and managed the company.

Tetsujiro, who was leading a fulfilling life as the de facto president of Marubeni Corporation, had a life-changing experience when he embarked on a six-month, thirteen-country tour of North America and Europe in 1928. While the main purpose of his trip was to ascertain conditions overseas in order to transition Marubeni Corporation from a textile wholesaler to a trading company, Testujiro also made an important discovery. He was deeply impressed by the many examples of prominent American citizens making large donations to their universities, as a way of returning a portion of the fruits of their personal success to society. After this voyage, Marubeni opened a store in Osaka and began focusing on international trade. The network of Marubeni branch stores expanded into China and India, and their product range diversified from textiles alone to include building materials, machinery, sundry goods and food products. The international trade division soon boasted the highest sales within the entire Marubeni Corporation.

In 1935, to celebrate his sixtieth birthday, Tetsujiro asked his hometown of Toyosato if he could donate the building, land and everything else necessary to rebuild the Toyosato Elementary School, his own alma mater. At the time, the school was in an inconvenient location and the building itself was small and in disrepair, so the relocation and reconstruction of the school was a major problem. To address this, Tetsujiro made a generous donation, providing a new location covering 40,000 square meters along the major Nakasendo Road, with a sports ground large enough for a straight 100-meter-race track.

The school building itself was made of chalk-white, iron-reinforced concrete. The central portion of the building was three floors, with a choir room and meeting rooms. There were also two-story wings extending from both sides to serve as classroom space.

The school was fully equipped with an auditorium, library, gymnasium, swimming pool, changing room, shower room and heating facilities, with additional classrooms for agriculture, science, and local crafts, and all the related educational supplies. William M. Vories, an American architect who contributed greatly to Japan, designed the new school. Through Vories' influence, the entire school adopted the American style, featuring lecture halls with benches and wide corridors. Compared to other Japanese elementary schools at the time, Toyosato Elementary School was so well equipped that it was even called, "the number one school in the East." The combined expenses of the building and land added up to 423,537 yen, ten times the budget of Toyosato at the time.

In the 1980s, the question of whether the school should be demolished or preserved became a major source of debate in Japanese society and was widely reported throughout Japan. Even then, Furukawa Tetsujiro was not mentioned even once. While his donation may have been a grand, public work of philanthropy widely praised at the time, just seventy years later it had receded into the mists of time to become an anonymous good deed.

The former building of Toyosato Elementary School

The former hall of the Toyosato Elementary School

Epilogue

This book was not written simply to share tales of the Ohmi merchants' glorious past, but rather to draw out the modern elements that can be found in their practices and management, and illustrate how those elements are linked to fundamental aspects of business today. The image of the Ohmi merchants, wearing sedge hats, *dochu-gappa* travelling cloaks, with wrist and leg gaiters, grass shoes and *tenbinbo* shoulder poles is so antiquated that one might think they have nothing to offer us in the modern age.

The point, however, has nothing to do with their external appearance. While it is difficult to separate commercial transactions from the unique culture, land, and age during which they were made, universal elements are hidden within those transactions that can surpass both space and time to be relevant today. The very fact that a significant number of the oldest companies in Japan today can trace their roots back over hundreds of years to the Ohmi merchants precisely illustrates the modern relevance of their legacy.

The Ohmi merchants, who have a history of 800 years, primarily turned their attention to making money in provinces outside Ohmi in the Edo period through itinerant trading and regional product rotation. Through these practices, they devised a number of unique management systems, and served as disseminators of culture in the rural regions of Japan. The practices and character of the Ohmi merchants led them to a management philosophy exemplified by "good for the seller, good for the buyer, good for the world," simplified to the phrase *sanpo-yoshi*, or three-way satisfaction. This management philosophy is their legacy to the world of management today.

While the prominent Ohmi merchants whose names are still known today may have expressed this shared philosophy in many different ways, they all emphasized the importance of considering a third party, society, in all commercial practices.

Looking at the endless series of corporate scandals occurring today, it is self-evident that the "good-for-the-world" perspective of the Ohmi merchants is critical to preventing the moral hazards that tend to accompany the pursuit of commercial profit. Even for the elite businessmen of today, who have traded the rustic *dochu-gappa* cloaks of long ago for sophisticated business suits, and bustle about our modern forests of glass and steel skyscrapers, it is essential that they constantly refine their sense of balancing the needs of work and society to achieve a new form of "good for the world" on a daily basis.

When we seek to leverage the *sanpo-yoshi* philosophy in the world of modern business, however, we must remind ourselves of the meaning of placing, "good for the seller" first. *Sanpo-yoshi* might seem a bit dubious if we jump to the conclusion that it still prioritizes the seller first among all parties. In interpreting *sanpo-yoshi* for the modern day, we should consider "good for the seller" to mean creating a positive work environment for everyone involved in selling the products of a business. In other words, it emphasizes employee satisfaction, which teaches a far more significant lesson than might be gained from a superficial interpretation of the phrase. Fundamentally, everyone would love to land a dream job where they can work with joy. If we create a positive work environment where employees can devote themselves to creating customer satisfaction, in other words achieving "good for the buyer," they will be able to feel the true satisfaction of working in a job that satisfies the needs of society, thus realizing "good for the world." Employee satisfaction leads to customer satisfaction, which results in satisfaction in society. The placement of "good for the seller" first in *sanpo-yoshi* represents the virtuous circle created by these three satisfactions.

I structured this book in the following manner: In the prologue I introduced the history and geography of the Ohmi region, and explained the factors that fostered the development of the Ohmi merchants. In Chapter 1, I presented the origins of the *sanpo-yoshi* spirit in the context of modern corporate social responsibility (CSR), which is now a highly publicized aspect of management. I then delved into the meaning of the "good for the world" aspect of *sanpo-yoshi*, and assessed the *sanpo-yoshi* philosophy as a truly made-in-Japan form of CSR, born from the country's unique history and culture. In Chapter 2, I presented the business and management practices of the Ohmi merchants, and their expansive vision, detailing the manner in which they kept their main residences in Ohmi, started off as itinerant traders, and went on to expand their territory and open branch stores throughout the key regions of Japan. In Chapter 3, based on the perspective that the essence of a company is established during its formative years, I gave a brief history of Ito Chubei I, the founder of Itochu and Marubeni, both of which have grown into massive general trading companies known throughout the world. In Chapter 4, I drew upon a series of essays I wrote between April 2001 and March 2004 for a magazine published by Shiga Bank, an offshoot of another bank originally founded by the Ohmi merchants, and selected and revised the contents of those essays into four categories: Insights from Management Philosophy, Insights from Management Methods, Insights from the Roles of Management, and Insights from History. In each section I analyzed the Ohmi merchants in relation to our modern times.

In describing the Ohmi merchants, I endeavored to write in a clear and concise style to best use the limited space and format available. I also focused on presenting concrete examples of the foresight and progressive nature of the Ohmi merchants, who devised unique business practices such as itinerant trading and regional product rotation, and thus served as forerunners of Japan's modern economy and business practices. To that end, I was forced to omit quotes from many historical materials that ideally should have been included, and to compensate for this, I included as many pictures as possible to spark the imagination of readers and allow them to truly gain a sense of the world of the Ohmi merchants.

Suenaga Kunitoshi
May 2018
Seiran-tei in western Kyoto

BIBLIOGRAPHY

Abashiri-shi shi, jokan (History of Abashiri City, vol. 1). Abashiri City, 1958.

Aoki Koji. *Hyakusho ikki sogo nenpyo* (Comprehensive Chronology of Peasant Riots). Sanichi Publishing Inc., 1971

Chogin Research Group (Ed.), *Henkakuki no shonin shihon: Ohmi shonin Chogin no kenkyu* (Merchant Capital in 19th-Century Japan: Research on Omi Merchant House Chogin). Yoshikawa Kobunkan, 1984.

Chojiya shoshi (The History of Chojiya). Chojiya Shoten Corporation, 1936.

Dai Nihon jinmei jisho (Japanese Biographical Dictionary). Naigai Shoseki, 1937.

Ebina Kenzo. *Nihonbashi no Ohmi shonin: Yanagiya Tonoike Uhei Toramatsu-ke no yonhyaku nen* (Ohmi Merchant of Nihonbashi: 400 Years of Yanagiya Tonoike Uhei Toramatsu). Shinhyoron Publishing, 2011.

Editorial Committee of the Nemuro and Chishima Encyclopedia of Historic Persons. *Nemuro, Chishima rekishi jinmei jiten* (Nemuro and Chishima Encyclopedia of Historic Persons). 2002.

Edojidai, hito zukuri fudoki Shiga (Edo Era: Record of the People and Culture of Shiga). Rural Culture Association Japan, 1996.

Egashira Tsuneharu. *Ohmi shonin Nakai-ke no kenkyu* (A Study of the Ohmi Merchant Family Nakai). 1965.

———. *Goshu shonin* (The Goshu merchants). Shibun-do, 1965.

Emori Susumu. *Hokkaido kinsei-shi no kenkyu: Bakuhan taisei to Ezochi* (Study of the History of Modern Hokkaido: Shogunate System and Ezo). Hokkaido Publication Project Center Ltd., 1982.

Gokasho-choshi shiryo shu I (Collection of Historical Materials on Gokasho Town, vol. 1). 1989.

Gokasho-choshi, dai 3 kanni (History of Gokasho Town, vol. 3). 1922.

Furukawa Tetsujiro (Ed.), *Arishihi no chichi* (The Life of my Father). 1937.

Fuse Zenjiro (Ed.), *Gendai Shiga-ken jinbutsu-shi ken, kon"* (Historical People Encyclopedia of Contemporary Shiga Prefecture, vol. 1 and 2). Shoryu-shya, 1919.

Harada Kan (Ed.), *Owari meisho zue* (Illustrations of Famous Sights in Owari). Nihon Meisho Zue Kankokai, 1919.

Hayashi Hiroshige. *Maboroshi no Minakai Hyakkaten* (The Mysterious Minakai Department Stores). Bansei-sha, 2004.

Hayashi Reiko. *Kanto no shoyu to orimono* (Soy Sauce and Textiles of the Kanto Region). Yoshikawa Kobunkan, 2003.

Hayashi Touichi. *Nagoya shonin-shi* (The History of Nagoya Merchants). Mid-Japan Economist, 1966.

———. *Kinsei Nagoya shonin no kenkyu* (Study of Early Modern Nagoya Merchants). University of Nagoya Press, 1994.

Hirase Mitsuyoshi. *Ohmi shonin* (Ohmi Merchants). Ohmi-shosho-kai, 1911.

Ioku Shigehiko and Nakanishi Satoru. *Shoyu jozogyo to chiiki no kogyoka: Takanashi Hyozaemon-ke no kenkyu* (Soy Sauce Brewing and Local Industrialization: Study of the Takanashi Hyozaemon Family). Keio University Press, 2016.

Inoue Masatomo (Ed.), *Ohmi shonin* (Ohmi Merchants). Shokei-do, 1890.

Ishii Kanji. *Kindai Nihon kinyu-shi josetsu* (History of the Beginnings of Modern Finance in Japan). University of Tokyo Press, 1999.

———. *Keizai hatten to ryogaesho kinyu* (Economic Development and Money Exchange Finance). Yuhikaku Publishing, 2007.

Ishii Kanji and Nakanishi Satoru, (Eds.) *Sangyoka to shoka keiei: Beikoku hiryosho Hiromike no kinsei · kindai* (Industrialization and the Management Practices of Merchants: Rice Fertilizer Business of the Hiromi Family in the Early Modern and Modern Times). University of Nagoya Press, 2006.

Ito Chubei Oh kaiso roku (The Reminiscence of Ito Chubei II). Itochu Corporation, 1974.

Itochu shoji hyakunen (100 years of Business, Itochu). Itochu Corporation, 1969.

Kadokawa Nihon chimei dai jiten (Geographical Dictionary of Japan by Kadokawa). Kadokawa Corporation, 1979.

Kagawa Takayuki. *Kinsei Edo shogyo-shi no kenkyu* (Study of the History of Early Modern Edo Commerce). Osaka University Press, 2012.

Kanada doho hatten-shi, dai 3 (History of the Development of Compatriots in Canada, vol. 3). Tairiku Nippo, 1924.

Kawakami Ujiro (Ed.), *Hachiman shogyo gojugo Nenshi* (55-year History of Shiga Prefecture Hachiman Commercial School). Shiga Prefecture Hachiman Commercial School 50th Anniversary Memorial Group, 1941.

Kanno Wataro. *Ohmi shonin no kenkyu* (A Study of Ohmi Merchants). Yuhikaku Publishing Co., Ltd., 1941.

Kiyama Minoru. *Kindai Nihon to Mitsui Bussan: Sogo shosha no kigen* (Modern Japan and Mitsui & Co., Ltd.: Origins of the General Trading Firm], Minerva Shobo, 2009.

Kumada Toru. *Rakuichi rakuza no tanjo* (Birth of Free Markets and Open Guilds). Iwanami Publication Service Center, 2000.

Marubeni Corporation. *Marubeni zenshi* (A Pre-History of Marubeni). Marubeni Corporation, 1977.

Matsui Kyuzaemon (Ed.), *Matsui Yuken-den* (The Life of Matsui Yuken). 1965.

Matsumoto Hiroshi (Ed.), *Ohmi Hino shonin no kenkyu, Yamanaka Hyoemon-ke no keiei to jigyo* (Study of the Ohmi Hino Merchants: Management Practices and Businesses of the Yamanaka Hyoemon Family). Nihon Keizai Hyoronsha, 2010.

Meiji jinmei jiten II (Biographical Dictionary of the Meiji period, vol. 2). Nihontosho Center Co., Ltd., 1988.

Miyamoto Matao. *Nihon kigyo keiei-shi kenkyu: Hito to seido to senryaku to* (Study of Japanese Corporate Management History: People, Systems, and Strategy), Yuhikaku Publishing, 2010.

Miyamoto Mataji. *Ono-gumi no kenkyu, zenyonkan* (Study of the Ono Group, vol. 1-4). Ohara Shinsei-sha, 1970.

———. *Kinsei shonin fudoki* (Landscape and History of Early Modern Merchants). Nippon Hyoron Sha, 1971.

Mori Kahei. *Iwate o tsukuru hitobito* (The People who Made Iwate). Modern Times Edition, Hosei University Press, 1974.

Morita Tsunenao (Ed.), *Josui Hirose Suketaro Oh* (The Life of Hirose Suketaro). 1940.

Myuzu Tsukamoto: 170-nen no ayumi (The 170-year History of Muse Tsukamoto). Tsukamoto Shoji Corporation, 1985.

Nakanishi Satoru. *Kinsei, Kindai Nihon no shijo kozo* (Japanese Market Structure in Early Modern and Modern Japan). University of Tokyo Press, 1998.

Nakayama, Gordon G. *Issei: Stories of Japanese Canadian Pioneers*. NC Press Limited Toronto, 1984.

Nakayama Jinshiro. *Kanada doho hatten taikan furoku* (Encyclopedia of the Development of Compatriots in Canada). 1921.

Nippon Seimei hyaku nenshi, jokan (100-year History of Nippon Life Insurance Company, vol. 1). Nippon Life Insurance Company, 1992.

Nippon Orimono Shimbun (Ed.), *Dai Nihon orimono nisen roppyaku nenshi* (The 2,600-year History of Japanese Textiles, vol 1). Nippon Orimono Shimbun Corporation, 1940.

Nishikawa Sangyo Co., Ltd. *Nishikawa yonhyaku nenshi kohon* (The 400-year History of Nishikawa). Nishikawa Sangyo Co., Ltd., 1966.

Nishikawa Tasaburo (Ed.), *Kaikoroku* (Retrospection record). Inanishi Corporation, 1927.

Ogawa Isao. *"Kigyo hatan to Kinyu hatan: Fu no rensa to risuku zoufuku no mekanizumu* (Corporate Bankruptcy and the Collapse of Financial Institutions: Mechanism behind Negative Chain Reactions and Risk Amplification). Kyushu University Press, 2002.

Ogura Eiichiro. *Goshu Nakai-ke choai no hou* (Management Accounting Method of the Nakai family). Minerva Shobo, 1962.

Ohashi Kinzo (Ed.), *Ohmi Kanzaki-gunshi ko, jokan* (History of Kanzaki County, Ohmi, vol. 1). Shiga-ken Kanzaki-gun Kyoikukai, 1928.

Ohmi Eichi-gunshi (History of Eichi County, Ohmi, vol. 3). 1929.

Ohmi Gamo-gunshi, dai 5 (History of Gamo County, Ohmi, vol. 5). Gamo County, 1922.

Ohmi Hachiman no rekishi, dai 5 kan shonin to akinai (History of Ohmihachiman, vol. 5 Merchants and Business). 2012

Ohmi Hino-choshi, kanchu (History of Hino Town, Ohmi, vol. 2). 1930.

Ohmi Hino no rekishi, dai 7 kani Hino shonin hen (History of Hino, Ohmi, vol. 7 Hino Merchant Edition). 2012.

Ohmi Nagahama-choshi, dai 3 maki (History of Nagahama District, Ohmi, vol. 3 chapter 1) Rinsen Book, Co., 1988.

Ono Zentaro. *Ishin no gosho Ono-gumi shimatsu* (Bankruptcy of the Ono group, Wealthy Merchants at the Time of the Meiji Restoration). Seia-bo, 1966.

Sakata Seiichi, *Harisu* (The Life of Townsend Harris). Yoshikawa Kobunkan, 1961.

Shiga Ginko goju nenshi (The 50-year History of Shiga Bank). Shiga Bank, Ltd., 1985.

Shiga-ken Hachiman-choshi (History of Hachiman District, Shiga Prefecture). Hachiman City, 1940.

Shiga-kenshi, dai 3 maki (History of Shiga Prefecture, vol. 3). Shiga Prefecture, 1928.

Shiga Prefectural Association of Education (Ed.), *Ohmi jinbutsu-shi* (History of the Ohmi people). Bunsen-do, 1917

Shiga Prefectural Economic Association (Ed.), *Ohmi shonin jiseki shashin-cho* (Photographic Record of Achievements by Ohmi merchants). 1930.

Shijo no shinka to shakai teki sekinin keiei ('Market Evolution' and CSR Management). Japan Association of Corporate Executives, 2003.

Shin Hokkaido-shi nenpyo (New Hokkaido Chronology). Hokkaido Publication Project Center Ltd., 1989.

Shinshu Otsu-shi shi, dai 5 kan (New Edition, History of Otsu City, vol. 5). Otsu City, 1982.

Shiraishi Takashi. *Nihonbashi Horidome Tokyo Orimono donya shiko* (Nihonbashi Horidome: Tokyo Textile Wholesale History). BUNSHINDOSHOTEN, 1994.

Suenaga Kunitoshi. *Kindai Ohmi shonin keieishi-ron* (Business History of Ohmi Merchants in 19th-Century Japan). Yuhikaku Publishing, 1997.

————. *Ohmi shonin: Gendai o ikinuku bijinesu no shishin* (The Ohmi merchants: Business Indicators for Surviving the Present Age). Chuokoron Shinsha, 2000.

————. *Nikkei Kanada imin no shakai-shi: Taiheiyo o watatta Ohmi shonin no matsuei-tachi* (Settlement Process of Japanese Canadians: Descendants of Ohmi Merchants who Crossed the Pacific). Minerva Shobo, 2010.

————. *Ohmi shonin, sanpo-yoshi keiei ni manabu* (Ohmi Merchants: Learning from Sanpo-yoshi Management). Minerva Shobo, 2011.

————. *Ohmi shonin to sanpo-yoshi: Gendai bijinesu ni ikiru chie* (Ohmi Merchants and Sanpo-yoshi: Wisdom for Survival in Modern Business). Institute of Moralogy, 2014.

Takahashi Kyuichi. *Meiji zenki chiho kinyukikan no kenkyu* (Study of Local Financial Institutions in the Early Meiji Era). Shinsei-sha, 1967.

Tsukakoshi Hiroshi. *Risutora nashi no nenrin keiei: Ii kaisha ha "toki o hakaru" yukkuri seicho* (Tree-Ring Management: Take the Long View and Grow Your Business Slowly). JPIC, 2015.

Uemura Masahiro. *Ohmi shonin no keiei-shi* (History of Ohmi Merchant Management). Seibundo Shuppan, 2000.

————. *Ohmi Hino shonin no keiei-shi: Ohmi kara Kanto e* (History of the Management Practices of the Ohmi Hino Merchants: From Ohmi to Kanto). Seibundo Shuppan, 2014.

Usami Hideki (Ed.), *Shodai Ito Chubei o tsuibosuru, arishihi no chichi, Marubeni, soshite shujin* (Remembering First Generation Ito Chubei: Father of the Early Days, Marubeni, and Proprietor), Seibundo Shuppan, 2012.

Watanabe Senjiro and Ohta Seiichiro. *Ohmi shonin no naijo, kokoku meifu-den* (Family Support for Ohmi Merchants: The Life of the Good Wife). 1935.

Yamanaka Takaki (Ed.), *Yamanaka-ke kashi* (History of the Yamanaka family). 1984.

Yao nihyaku goju nenshi (The 250-year History of Yao). Yao Department Store Co., Ltd. Yao Head Office, Memorial Chichibu, 1998.

Yasuoka Shigeaki, Fujita Teiichiro, and Ishikawa Kenjiro (Eds.), *Ohmi shonin no keiei isan: Sono saihyoka* (Ohmi Merchant's Heritage: A Reassessment). Dobunkan, 1992.

INDEX

ABOUT THE AUTHOR

SUENAGA Kunitoshi
Born in Fukuoka Prefecture in 1943 and grew up in Saga Prefecture. After graduating from the Faculty of Economics at Doshisha University, he received his doctorate in economic research from the Graduate School of Economics at the same university. Holding the title Doctor of Economics, he served as a professor at the Faculty of Economics at Kyoto Sangyo University and went on to become a professor in the Faculty of Economics at Doshisha University. Currently, he is an emeritus professor at Doshisha University and the director of the Ohmi Merchant Local Museum (Foundation).

SPECIALTIES:
Japanese Economic and Business History

PUBLICATIONS:
Kindai Ohmi shonin keieishi-ron [Business History of Ohmi Merchants in 19th-Century Japan], Yuhikaku Publishing, 1997

Ohmi shonin: Gendai o ikinuku bijinesu no shishin [The Ohmi Merchants: Business Indicators for Surviving the Present Age] Chuokoron-Shinsha, 2000

Nikkei Kanada imin no shakai-shi: Taiheiyo o watatta Ohmi shonin no matsuei-tachi [Settlement Process of Japanese Canadians: Descendants of Ohmi Merchants who Crossed the Pacific] Minerva Shobo, 2010

Ohmi shonin, sanpo-yoshi keiei ni manabu [Ohmi Merchants, Learning from Sanpo-yoshi Management], Minerva Shobo, 2011

Ohmi shonin to sanpo-yoshi: Gendai bijinesu ni ikiru chie [The Ohmi Merchants and Sanpo-yoshi: Wisdom for Survival in Modern Business], Institute of Moralogy, 2014

JOINT PUBLICATIONS:
Henkakuki no shonin shihon: Ohmi shonin Chogin no kenkyu [Merchant Capital in Nineteenth-Century Japan: Research on Ohmi Merchant House Chogin], Yoshikawa Kobunkan, 1984

ABOUT THE TRANSLATOR

Larry Greenberg grew up in New York and came to Japan after graduating from Williams College in 1985. While studying at the Japanese Language Institute of Nichibei Kaiwa Gakuin he began a career in translation that led to him establishing Urban Connections, a leading translation company. Over the course of three decades Larry has managed hundreds of employees from many countries in a diverse multinational and multicultural setting where effective communication is essential.

（英文版）近江商人学入門—CSR の源流「三方よし」改訂版

The Story of Japan's Ohmi Merchants: The Precept of Sanpo-yoshi

2019年5月27日　第1刷発行

著　者　末永國紀
訳　者　ラーリ・グリーンバーグ
発行所　一般財団法人 出版文化産業振興財団
　　　　〒101-0051 東京都千代田区神田神保町3-12-3
　　　　電話　03-5211-7282（代）
　　　　ホームページ　http://www.jpic.or.jp/

印刷・製本所　大日本印刷株式会社

Heterick Memorial Library
Ohio Northern University

DUE	RETURNED	DUE	RETURNED
1.		13.	
2.		14.	
3.		15.	
4.		16.	
5.		17.	
6.		18.	
7.		19.	
8.		20.	
9.		21.	
10.		22.	
11.		23.	
12.		24.	

Heterick Memorial Library
Ohio Northern University
Ada, Ohio 45810